A **PICTURE**
OF **BRITAIN**

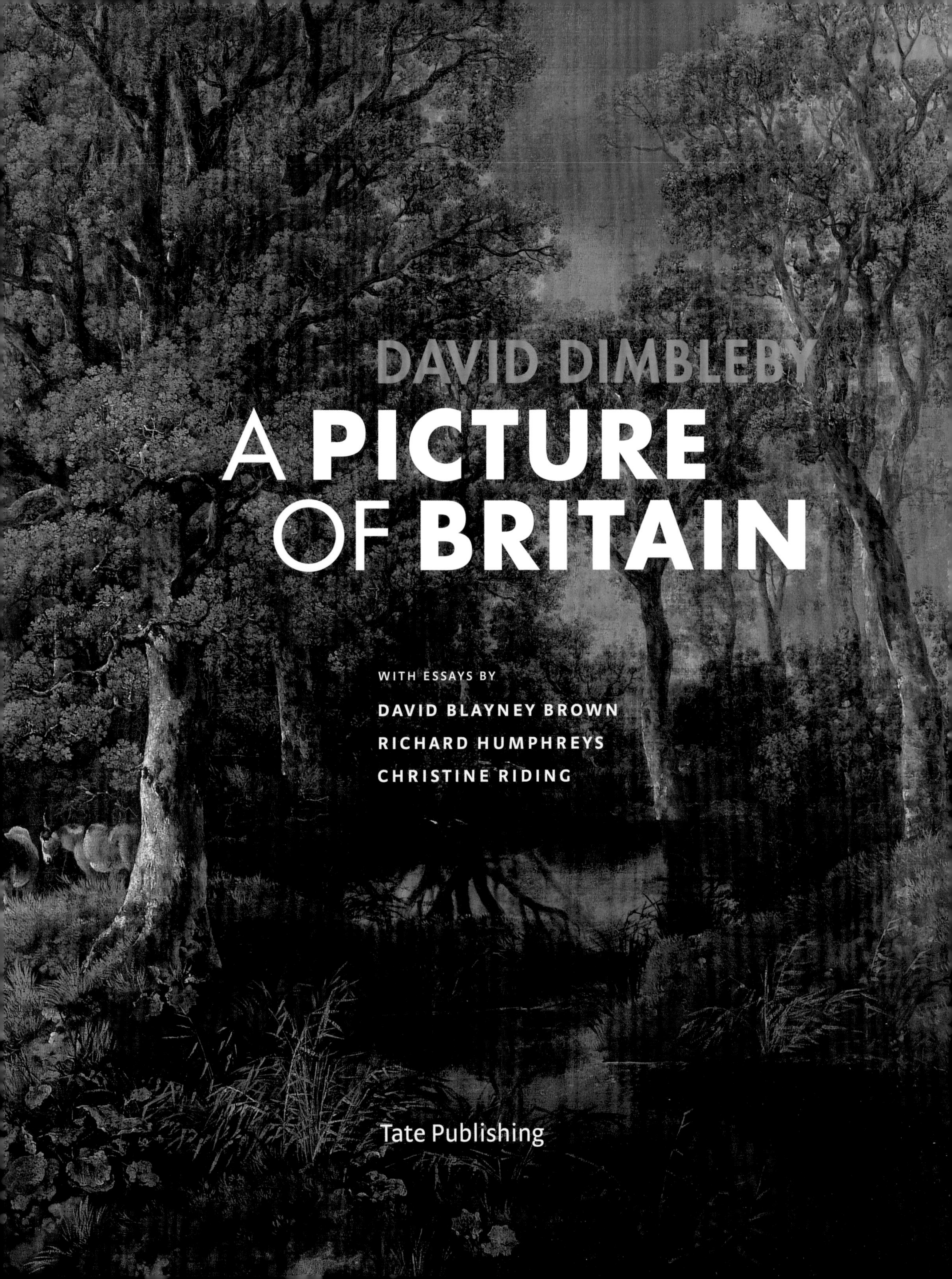

DAVID DIMBLEBY

A PICTURE OF BRITAIN

WITH ESSAYS BY

DAVID BLAYNEY BROWN

RICHARD HUMPHREYS

CHRISTINE RIDING

Tate Publishing

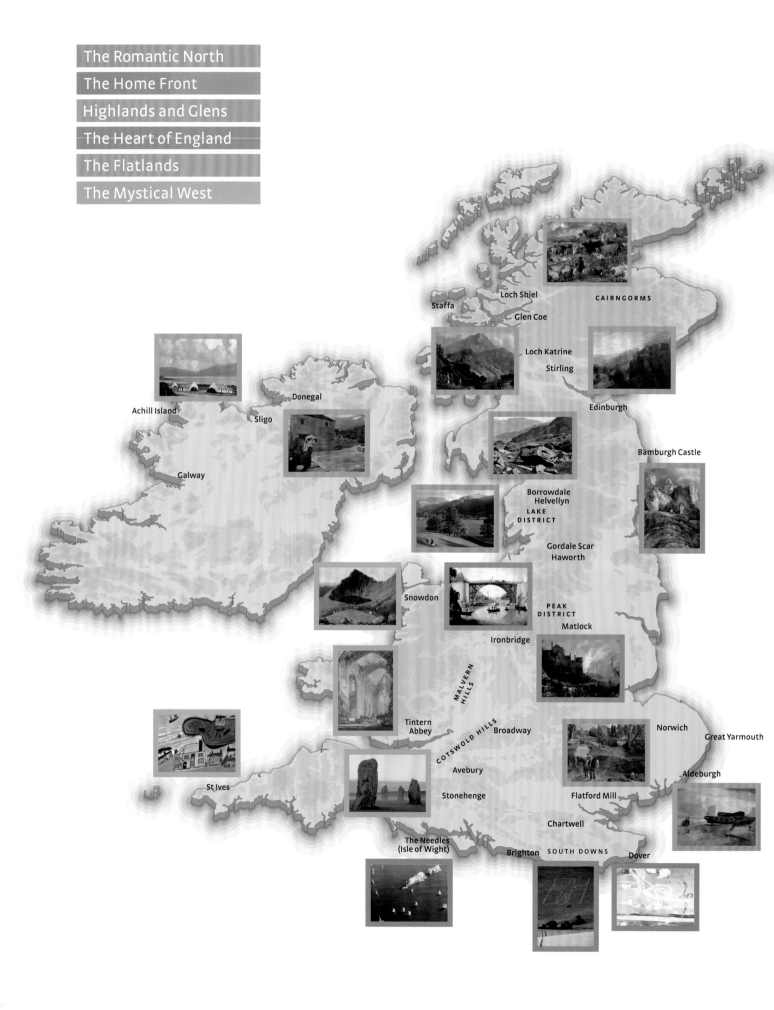

The Romantic North

The Home Front

Highlands and Glens

The Heart of England

The Flatlands

The Mystical West

Loch Shiel

Staffa

CAIRNGORMS

Glen Coe

Loch Katrine

Stirling

Edinburgh

Donegal

Achill Island

Sligo

Bamburgh Castle

Galway

Borrowdale
Helvellyn
LAKE
DISTRICT

Gordale Scar
Haworth

Snowdon

PEAK
DISTRICT

Matlock

Ironbridge

MALVERN
HILLS

Tintern
Abbey

Norwich

Broadway

Great Yarmouth

COTSWOLD HILLS

St Ives

Avebury

Aldeburgh

Stonehenge

Flatford Mill

Chartwell

The Needles
(Isle of Wight)

Brighton   SOUTH DOWNS

Dover

Contents

Foreword

The British countryside has been a source of deep pleasure, intense national and regional pride, and public debate and controversy for hundreds of years. Visual artists have been at the heart of the phenomenon throughout this time, creating, defining and reacting to the ideas, feelings and images which form the complex thing we call 'the British Landscape' – and the myriad reactions we all have to it.

A Picture of Britain is a unique collaboration between the BBC and Tate Britain, aiming to present to a broad audience the enormously rich heritage of the finest British rural landscape art of the last two centuries or more. The project has been conceived over a two-year period by gallery curators and educators, television producers and researchers working together in a uniquely close and collaborative way. The outcome has been a landmark television series on BBC1 presented by David Dimbleby, a major exhibition at Tate Britain, a number of other television and radio programmes, public events, on-line initiatives from both Tate and the BBC – and this publication. Between them Tate Britain and the BBC have created something which reaches out to everyone who lives in or visits Britain and who wishes to enjoy and to understand the nation's physical and emotional character through its landscape.

The television series, exhibition and book are all organised around six regions which cover the varied landscape of Britain and the many different artistic responses to it. While the project cannot cover all places and all artists, it does aim at providing a series of linked stories focused on the particular locations where some of Britain's greatest artists have found their inspiration. *A Picture of Britain* draws a map of Britain as seen through the eyes of its artists: from Turner in Scotland to Paul Nash in the South of England, from Richard Wilson in Wales to John Constable in East Anglia and from Joseph Wright in the 'Heart of England' to L. S. Lowry in the industrial North.

But *A Picture of Britain* also goes beyond painting, to include photography and poster art, for example, as well as the literature, poetry and music that has helped shaped our vision of Britain. Meanwhile *A Digital Picture of Britain* on BBC4 will extend the project into the modern day, by inviting both professional photographers and the public to create their own pictures of Britain through the medium of digital photography.

We hope that *A Picture of Britain* is just the start of a new approach to collaboration in which major national institutions such as the BBC and Tate come together to give the public the benefit of their enormous combined resources of knowledge, skills, and technical expertise. Together we can all share and enjoy the rich artistic heritage and culture which inspires and informs us both as individuals and as a nation.

STEPHEN DEUCHAR
Director, Tate Britain

MARK HARRISON
Creative Director, BBC Arts

A Picture of Britain

DAVID DIMBLEBY

In our crowded islands, landscape has become a luxury. Most of us live in cities, towns or suburbs. It is possible day after day, week after week, to see only our immediate surroundings – the street we live in, the view from the bus or commuter train, or glimpses of open space from a morning traffic jam on the motorway. Despite this, the countryside has a powerful hold on our imagination. At the latest count seven million people visit the country every weekend to look at the scenery, picnic at a famous beauty spot, or walk barefoot along the beach. We find comfort in the countryside, take pleasure in its sights and sounds, and are excited by its storms and sunsets. It seems natural to us, but our ways of seeing it are not natural. We have acquired our taste for it, learned partly from the generations that came before us, and our taste is constantly evolving.

For centuries much of the countryside we now enjoy visiting was seen as inhospitable. It was believed that truly civilised life was only possible in the towns. Except for the wealthy, the countryside was a place of unremitting toil and few visited it for pleasure. It took the vision of artists and writers, particularly over the past three hundred years, to lead people towards an understanding of its natural beauty, to see things they had never really looked at, and so come to realise that the British landscape was to be cherished.

In his book *Landscape into Art*, the art historian Kenneth Clark points out that in the early Middle Ages St Anselm described the pleasure found in natural things, flowers and birdsong as dangerous to the soul, enticing believers away from the true path to salvation. It was only gradually that the Church, the dominant cultural force in Britain, allowed the depiction of natural objects in churches – carvings of animals or bunches of grapes – to be enjoyed for themselves.

Writers and poets such as Chaucer and Shakespeare saw beauty in landscape long before most painters began to record it. Artists came to the representation of landscape very late and their first attempts look rather contrived to our modern eyes. The tradition of painting ruled that the

John Knox (1778–1845), *Landscape with Tourists at Loch Katrine* c.1820s (detail)

9

proper subject for art was man, and not man set in the reality of his daily life, but man heroic as revealed in the great stories taken from the Bible or from classical mythology. Landscape for its own sake was not thought worth serious and undivided attention.

All this began to change in the seventeenth century, most strikingly under the influence of the French painter Claude Lorrain. Claude painted landscape for its own sake, albeit with strict rules about how elements should be depicted. There had to be a proper foreground, usually of dark overhanging trees, and often with allegorical figures disporting themselves on green sward. The eye was then led back into the middle distance, helped by carefully placed rivers or bridges, hills and mountains. This created what has become known as the 'classical landscape' based on the countryside around Rome where Claude lived, full of mythological figures and ancient ruins. You cannot look at a Claude as you can at a Constable and recognise the place that he has painted. Brilliant and exciting though his work is, it is a formal reconstruction of elements of landscape rather than what we would think of as landscape itself.

I blithely write 'what we would think of as landscape itself' when what we think of as landscape changes all the time. Under the influence of Claude the first tourists, setting out with all their baggage to sites recommended by the guidebook, would often carry a 'Claude glass'. This was a mirror designed to be held up to the view which could then be observed not in the raw, but through the looking glass. The user stood with his back to the landscape adjusting the mirror until a perfect Claudian image was achieved. The viewer was looking at the scenery not through his own eyes but through Claude's. An increasing number of tourists in the mid-eighteenth century would travel with the newly developed watercolours, and paint or draw what they saw not from life but from the mirror.

As I have travelled around these islands I have often thought of this image of the eighteenth-century traveller and of how absurd it seems. But gradually I came to understand how our view of nature has been formed, at least in part. It was while I was walking in a wood near my home under the South Downs that I first had an inkling of the influence Claude must have had. A muddy track leads through a scruffy wood towards the Downs. To the left the ground slopes towards the site of an old, now overgrown, chalk pit. The soil is poor, a scree of chalk. The south-westerly gales accelerate as they reach this wood, channelled

Claude Lorrain (1600–1682), *Landscape with Hagar and the Angel* 1646

through a gap in the hills, and wreak havoc. Everywhere there are dead branches or the trunks of huge fallen beeches, their roots sticking in the air still clogged with earth. To one side is a fine view down the slope of the hill towards the low weald, but I kept finding my eye drawn back to the damaged wood and to one tree trunk in particular covered in green moss and jutting down towards the path.

One day, wondering why I found this particular tree so interesting, I remembered a painting by Graham Sutherland I had always admired. It is called *Green Tree Form: Interior of Woods* (1940), and shows a fallen green tree jutting out at the same angle as my tree. I realised that without the memory of that Sutherland I might well have passed by my tree without a second glance.

It was irritating to think that Sutherland had made me take notice of the tree, that it had not been spontaneous, had not sprung pristine from my imagination but had been derived from his. He had been there first, but once an idea of what is beautiful has been implanted it is hard to dislodge. Anyone who has walked the Downs as I often do and who has seen any paintings of the Downs cannot fail to be seduced by the images they have seen: the Downs like Atlantic rollers thundering in from the sea; the Downs as abstract shapes, angular fields, some green, some striped with plough; the Downs marked out by chalk tracks winding up the hills and disappearing over their crests. And who could forget the Downs as the setting for Paul Nash's wartime paintings of vapour trails in the sky while fighter planes engage in a dog-fight high above? However much you want to have your own private image of the Downs you cannot escape what others have shown you. The eye is conditioned to see what it has been told to look at – just like the tourists with their Claude glass.

I found it easier to accept that what we see in landscape does not spring from our own natural instincts but from what we have learned over generations when I went to the Lake District. Today the Lakes are the focus of a tourist industry. All summer long coaches and cars grind their way along narrow roads pausing long enough for us to exclaim over Windermere or Ullswater, or visit Wordsworth's cottage and try to look at daffodils through his eyes. But in 1720 Daniel Defoe travelled through the Lakes and described it as the 'the wildest, most barren and frightful' of any country he had been through. The high hills (which we call mountains) were 'terrible and inaccessible', their tops 'covered with snow seemed to

Graham Sutherland (1903–1980), *Green Tree Form: Interior of Woods* 1940

tell us all the pleasant part of England was at an end'. No-one would think of visiting such a place for pleasure.

I had an inkling of what Defoe meant when I walked up the lower slopes of Helvellyn in winter. At just over three thousand feet (950 metres) it is the third highest hill in England. Within an hour of setting off we were in a snowstorm. The peaks were hidden in swirling cloud. The wind brought the temperature down to -18°c. Fortunately, I was in the good company of three mountain rescue experts to whom this was nothing, but for my part my cheeks were frozen and my left ear, exposed to the icy blasts, felt as though it had been sliced off. I empathised with van Gogh.

My guides produced curious mushroom-shaped sheets of brightly coloured plastic. Four of us stood under this dome holding the edges of it behind us. On a command we all sat down at once, like musical chairs, and were squatting on the ground protected from the snow by the sheet. It would have worked well except that I was sitting where the ground fell away and kept falling out. Defoe and those other early travellers had no such protection nor such skilled guides. No wonder they thought it a frightening place.

But the disdain for the Lakes was not just because they could be in-hospitable and even dangerous. They still can be for those who are not careful. It was that no-one had yet begun to see them in a different light as places with a particular and spectacular beauty.

It is possible to trace this transformation over the past three hundred years and see how our perceptions have been altered by the imagination of others. One of the first was a local clergyman, Dr John Brown, who

"Daniel Defoe travelled through the Lakes and described it as 'the wildest, most barren and frightful' of any country ... I had an inkling of what Defoe meant when I walked up the lower slopes of Helvellyn in winter"

became known as the Columbus of the Lakes. In 1752 he wrote a letter about his annual visits to Keswick which was published as a pamphlet and sold to early tourists. His choice of words strikes us now as over-dramatic: the scene united 'beauty, horror and immensity' and 'a sense of danger was still never far away'. He analysed the appeal of 'rocks and cliffs of stupendous height, hanging broken over the lake in horrible grandeur', and from the top of a hill he looked over 'an immense and awful picture . . . the image of a tempestuous sea of mountains'.

Brown's language struck a chord with a generation of travellers. Within a few years a tourist industry was burgeoning, threatening to overwhelm the wilderness which the visitors had come to see. Hotels and inns opened. Boat-hire businesses sprung up. Horse-drawn carriages on their way to the most popular sites created traffic jams so familiar to the modern tourist. A guide to the Lakes was published in 1778 which identified the twenty-one best viewpoints, many of them places still mentioned in guide books today. Thomas West (another priest incidentally, a Jesuit missionary) describes in meticulous detail what to observe from each of his chosen spots. I went to several of them with his book in hand. It was like walking in the company of an artist who could point out subtleties of colour and shape I might otherwise have missed; though sometimes, as one of his early detractors pointed out, it would have been better 'if the descriptions were not so highly wrought'.

But most intriguing of the pioneers who wanted to open his readers' eyes to a beauty they had not perceived was yet another clergyman, William Gilpin (1724–1804). Apart from teaching, building a school and poorhouse in his parish and publishing lives of, among others, Hugh Latimer and Thomas Cranmer, Gilpin found time to write five books of his summer tours illustrated with his own aquatint drawings. If our greatest painters, Turner and Constable, influenced the way other great artists saw landscape, Gilpin led a generation of amateurs to see landscape in a particular way. He describes, sometimes in almost comic detail, how to compose a landscape drawing or painting, with strict rules for the aspiring artist. His aim is to lead them towards 'the picturesque', a way of taking from nature the elements that are most satisfying to the eye and through the eye to the soul. Faced with the confusion of scenery the artist should ensure that there are craggy mountains in the distance, not with smooth curved tops, but jagged. There should be a lake in the middle distance and

. . . the imagination is apt to whisper, What glorious scenes might here be made, if these stubborn materials could yield to the judicious hand of art! – And, to say the truth, we are sometimes tempted to let the imagination loose among them.
WILLIAM GILPIN, 1786

Thomas Hearne (1744–1817), *Sir George Beaumont and Joseph Farington Sketching a Waterfall c.1777* (detail)

Edwin Smith (1912–1971), *Gordale Scar, Yorkshire* 1969

the foreground should contain trees, rocks and cascades of water. He was very particular about the colour of the rocks. Grey was preferable to red as it set off green foliage more effectively. Isolated buildings in the middle distance were also acceptable, but only if they were partially in ruins. Animals, too, had to be carefully selected and arranged to ensure a perfect composition. Gilpin admitted that horses are more noble than cows, but their disadvantage for the artist is that they are too soft and rounded to make a satisfying subject. Better draw cows, with their angular shape, but make sure you do not put in too many or they will risk dominating the scene. Three is the ideal number, he suggested, either in a group, or two together and one slightly apart. Sheep are always acceptable, as long as they have not been recently shorn.

Gilpin had his detractors and at times seems even to be sending himself up, but his influence on the way a generation of amateur artists came to see landscape is telling. Before the invention of the camera, most educated people had learned to draw and often sketched as they travelled. Drawing is demanding. It forces you to focus on what you see and to interpret it. What Gilpin taught with his ten commandments for the artist was that the landscape itself is only the raw material of a drawing. Not everything you see can be put down on paper. You must learn to single out the features you want to draw attention to and ignore what does not fit. His own complex prescription may seem risible today but his approach to landscape is revealing because it gives an insight into how artists make use of landscape and how each of us comes to see landscape in our own way.

The reason landscape is not an inferior art form, as it was so long thought to be, is that landscape no less than the human form repays attention. To our generation, which has been trained to accept that every-thing from baked bean tins to unmade beds can be the object of the artist's attention, this may seem so obvious that it is barely worth stating. But two hundred years ago to take landscape seriously was to depart radically from conventional taste. We should be grateful for the pioneers who made British landscape painting a unique contribution to art.

Why Britain in particular? Holland's vast skies and flat lands defined by canals and punctuated by windmills gave rise to a way of painting which preceded the British interest in landscape. But Britain, as I realised travel-ling from one breathtaking view to another, has a prodigious variety of scenery and an infinite variety of light which changes the way that scenery

…it cannot be supposed that every scene … is *correctly picturesque* … many irregu-larities, many deformities, must exist, which a practised eye would wish to correct. Mountains are sometimes crouded – their sides are often bare, when contrast requires them to be wooded …
WILLIAM GILPIN, 1786

looks. It is a rich source of inspiration not just for the trained eye of the artist but for all of us. We still travel to lovely places for inspiration, albeit in the comfort of heated cars, playing our favourite music. Nature takes us out of our supposedly controllable world with all the technical innovations that now define our daily life into a world we cannot control, which obeys its own laws and which was here before us and will be here after us. That is why it is so important to us even if we only make occasional forays to observe it at first hand. As we cover great tracts of our islands with motorways and leisure centres, shopping malls and new housing, it is more vital than ever to nurture those places which offer a different vision.

A government minister, defending the explosion of development taking place in southern England, told me that when he flew by helicopter he was astonished at how much of Britain was still green. From a helicopter that may be so, but most of us cannot enjoy that luxury. He was right though. If you look for it, ours is still not just a green and pleasant land, but a land of barren moorland, craggy peaks, wild cliffs and tempestuous seas. To immerse ourselves in it restores not just a sense of balance but of awe and wonder at the world we live in. Our rich tradition of landscape painting is an invaluable and stimulating guide on that journey.

The Romantic North

There are many countries where it is forbidden to take photographs of military installations, airports and even bridges. The unwary tourist can find himself in jail for the night – or worse – for breaking the law. But before photography, drawing was the only method of recording information. Soldiers learned to draw as part of their military training. So the artist Francis Place's arrest in 1678 should

have come as no surprise. At a time when travel was uncomfortable if not dangerous Place's quirky hobby was to travel throughout Britain drawing as he went. He was careless about his safety. 'We trudge on,' he once said, 'never enquiring after anything but where the best ale is'. His movements aroused suspicion however, fuelled by rumours of a Catholic plot against Charles II.

He was arrested and thrown into jail: our first landscape artist risking torture and even execution for his art. Friends came to the rescue, vouching for him and for his innocent pursuit, and he continued painting until he died at the age of eighty-one.

Place was the first British artist to use painting to show more than the dry topographical detail of a scene.

> "I have come to share the same excitement and exhilaration that early travellers felt when they wandered those wild uplands, a landscape that lends itself to a taste for the spectacular, the dramatic, and the fearful."

Thomas Girtin (1775–1802), *Bamburgh Castle, Northumberland c.*1797–9

His innovation was to exaggerate what he saw, to point out the key features in heightened form and so capture not just the dull formal outlines of what he observed but also its character and spirit. Place painted Bamburgh Castle, the same rugged coastline of Northumberland later captured by the young Turner and by Thomas Girtin. Many years ago I saw a Girtin watercolour for sale in a gallery for a few pounds when a Turner would have sold for a hundred times the price. Since then, Girtin's place in landscape painting is secure. We have come to recognise what Turner saw in him. He is supposed to have said, 'If Tom Girtin had lived, I would have starved'.

As a southerner – born, bred and educated well below the Watford Gap – I have always been slightly in awe of northerners, accepting the image they cultivate of themselves as tougher, blunter, less effete than the soft southerner. For many years I felt more at home in continental Europe than the North, where I felt a foreigner. Time and much travel through the North has eroded that prejudice. I have come to share the same excitement and exhilaration that early travellers felt when they wandered those wild uplands, a landscape that lends itself to a taste for the spectacular, the dramatic, and the fearful.

Eighteenth-century tourists found a country more savage than we see today. Partly it is because we are cosseted on our travels and many of the places we go to see have been

Gordale Scar

packaged by tourist boards keen to make everywhere accessible. Early travellers seemed to have a greater sense of adventure and a greater willingness to seek out thrills where they could be found and to invent them if they could not. On a cold February day I stood on the deck of an elegant old passenger boat in the middle of Ullswater in the Lake District. Our plan was to fire a cannon from the deck and listen to the echo rebounding six or more times from the hills and valleys around us. This was a favourite excursion two hundred years ago. After several attempts we found a spot where the echo did come back at us from all sides. We were less successful with our four French horn players. The eighteenth-century

guidebook said the sound would be like a thousand symphonies. The musicians played bravely, fingers frozen, but the wind was too much for them, and no echo came.

The Lakes have long been the backdrop for powerful emotions. Your taste may run to Wordsworth and his Daffodils ('the worst poem in the English language', a fourteen-year-old complained to me). Or maybe you prefer Coleridge, high on opium and despairing of his failing marriage and floundering writing career, abandoning himself to the worst the mountains of the Lakes could offer. He wrote of his hands torn by jagged rocks, his eyes swelling blood red in the stinging wind, leaping from narrow ledge to narrow ledge in his descent of Scafell. 'The first rock climber' some mountaineers call him, though his careless abandon is not an example today's climbers would extol, admire it though they may.

To understand this landscape, and to share the excitement the first visitors felt, it is best to re-enter their world, to see it through their eyes, to accept a little exaggeration of height and depth, both of the world around you and of your own emotions. You may then be able to rekindle the sense of awe which can otherwise seem so alien to our modern eyes and ears.

The farther I ascend from animated Nature, from men, and cattle, & the common birds of the woods, & fields, the greater becomes in me the Intensity of the feeling of Life ... I do not think it possible, that any bodily pains could eat out the love & joy, that is so substantially part of me, towards hills, & rocks, and steep waters!

Samuel Taylor Coleridge, *Letters*, 14 January 1803

'Man, Nature and Society'

DAVID BLAYNEY BROWN

How do we make sense of a region stretching from Cumbria to Northumberland, Lancashire to Yorkshire, and embracing cities and wilderness, mills and mines, moors and fells, mountains and lakes? How do we picture it? Are pictures even what come to mind? Do we think of the first railways, the Lindisfarne Gospels, William Wordsworth or *Wuthering Heights*, J. B. Priestley or Catherine Cookson? At Whitby might we remember Captain Cook or Bram Stoker's *Dracula*? For a cruise on Coniston Water would we choose the *Ruskin* or the *Ransome*? How important are people to our sense of place? Who are the figures in the landscape? To raise even a few such questions is to realise the complexity of our regional awareness.

OPPOSITE
Atkinson Grimshaw (1836–1893),
*Bowder Stone, Borrowdale c.*1863–8
(detail)

Stanley Royle (1888–1961), *Sheffield from Wincobank Wood* 1923

The North has given us two of our most powerful metaphors for Britain – the workshop of the world and the wilderness. In order for the first to exist, the second had to be conquered. This is one story of the North. Stanley Royle's *Sheffield from Wincobank Wood* of 1923 depicts the steel-works of the Lower Don Valley in their smoke-belching prime. This is the image of the North that we often oppose to that of the South. But it is a long way away from other depictions of the North – Julian Cooper's *Large Honister Crag*, for example, a study of the mountain near his home. For such a scene to be appreciated, it first had to be 'discovered'. This is another story, and neither story begins or ends with pictures such as these.

Julian Cooper's mountain paintings are painted from a climber's experience of feel and grip. They aim to reconnect us with nature and the landscape, a link that the artist feels has been lost.

Julian Cooper (born 1947) *Large Honister Crag* 2003–4

Atkinson Grimshaw (1836–1893), *Bowder Stone, Borrowdale c.1863–8*

The most prominent feature in Royle's view today is a shopping centre. The Industrial Revolution now seems a passing chapter in the long dialogue between man and nature that is the real story of the North. It is a story conducted as much in words as in pictures – hesitantly at first and then perhaps more vividly than anywhere else in our country.

When the aristocratic adventuress Celia Fiennes visited the Lake District and other parts of the North in 1698 as part of her 'great journey' around Britain, she dismissed it as 'mostly rocks'. The urbane Daniel Defoe, in his *Tour through the Whole Island of Great Britain* (1724–7), thought Liverpool and Leeds wonders of the world, but the Pennines beyond civilisation and Westmorland the 'wildest, most barren and frightful' place he had ever seen. Their contemporary, the York-based Francis Place, was sufficiently unusual in drawing his native land as to get himself arrested. It would have been inconceivable to these early travellers that one day an artist would bother to visit the Bowder Stone in its remote location in Borrowdale, let alone paint it with the microscopic accuracy that Atkinson

Grimshaw brought to his work of the 1860s. Conscious only of inconveniences between places they actually wanted to visit, they had no interest in natural features and no concept of landscape as scenery. But by 1778, when Defoe's book went into the last of nine reprints (not to reappear until 1927), the British had discovered these things. The North was their *locus classicus* and the Lake District their holy grail.

PICTURESQUE AND SUBLIME

It was only a matter of time before the classically educated elite of eighteenth-century Britain began to look for an Arcadia at home. Cumbrians took a lead. Writing to Lord Lyttelton, probably in 1753, the Cambridge Don Dr John Brown famously associated '*Beauty, Horror* and *Immensity*', and the three most popular old master painters of the age, Claude Lorrain, Nicolas Poussin and Salvator Rosa, with the area round Keswick. Meanwhile, in his *Analytical Enquiry into our Ideas of the Sublime and Beautiful* (1757), Edmund Burke contrasted the appearance of landscapes that inspired the awe and admiration associated with the two conditions – to be found in abundance in the Lake District. Brown's observations, together with Thomas Gray's vivid letters, written during a Lakeland visit in 1769 and subsequently edited as a 'journal' (1775), were printed in the second (1780) edition of Thomas West's *Guide to the Lakes*. This was dedicated to a new audience, 'Lovers of Landscape Studies', whom it directed to particular 'stations' to admire the mountains and reflecting water that so obligingly fell into symmetry. Soon more books appeared to teach readers how to look at landscape, such as William Gilpin's *Observations, relative chiefly to Picturesque Beauty* . . . (1786; previously circulated in manuscript), based mainly on the 'Mountains and Lakes' of England, or Uvedale Price's thoughtful *Essays on the Picturesque* (1794). Technology, too, was brought to bear. Visitors often carried their 'Claude glass', to view the scenery through the perspective of their favourite painter.

Price despised the fashion for prospects. Thomas Rowlandson and William Combe sent it up. Their brilliant spoof of Gilpin's gushing text, which they called *The Tour of Dr Syntax in Search of the Picturesque* (1813), ridiculed the whole generation of idle rich now flocking to the Lake District – 'heartless fops', as Thomas Love Peacock described them in his

Thomas Hearne (1744–1817),
*Sir George Beaumont and Joseph
Farington Sketching a Waterfall* c.1777

Towne's watercolour was made during a Lake District tour in 1786, when the artist based himself in Ambleside.

Francis Towne (1739–1816), *Waterfall near Ambleside* 1786

novel *Melincourt* (1817), 'who take their fashionable autumn tour, to gape at rocks and waterfalls, for which they have neither eyes nor ears'. It would be wrong to number Sir George Beaumont among these visitors, however. He was an artist, friend and patron of both artists and writers. He gave his drawing of a waterfall at Keswick to the poet Wordsworth, while his painter friend Thomas Hearne drew him, with another colleague, Joseph Farington, balancing their easels on the rocks to paint a cascade at Lodore. No serious artist could now avoid making a Lakeland tour, or joining in the aesthetic debates of the time. Philip James de Loutherbourg favoured a

John Crome (1768–1821), *Slate Quarries* c.1802–5

Gilpinesque view, as schematic as Francis Towne's watercolours are lapidary and precise. John Glover's Lakeland scenes show why he thought himself an English Claude. The Norwich artist John Crome struck a sublime note with his bleak *Slate Quarries*. Not all artists found their voice among the lakes and mountains. Constable tried in 1806, but 'the solitude of mountains oppressed his spirits'. Samuel Palmer avoided 'lumpen mountains and leaden lakes' – and those who wrote about them. But many did, and well beyond the age that made them fashionable.

NATURAL HISTORY

By 1808, a visitor to a London exhibition could feel like 'an outside passenger on a mail-coach making a picturesque and picturizing journey to the North ... Mountains and cataracts, rivers, lakes, and woods, deep romantic glens and sublime sweeps of country, engage his eye.' A Lakeland visit was often combined with a wider tour of northern England. Turner's itinerary in 1797, extending to Yorkshire, Durham and Northumberland, the Borders of Scotland and Lancashire, took in both natural scenery and antiquities. This new 'Grand Tour' soon became a substitute for the traditional aristocratic tour of Europe closed by the Napoleonic Wars. A single county, Yorkshire, could keep an artist busy for years with its rivers, moors and dales, castles, abbeys and cathedrals, and great estates whose proprietors, like Edward Lascelles at Harewood or Walter Fawkes of Farnley,

And at last fortune wills that the lad's true life shall begin; and one summer's evening, after various wonderful stage-coach experiences on the north road ... he finds himself sitting alone among the Yorkshire hills ... Peace at last ... Freedom at last ... Loveliness at last ... Here is something He has made which no one has marred.
JOHN RUSKIN on Turner, *Modern Painters*, 1860

James Ward (1769–1859), *Gordale Scar (A View of Gordale in the Manor of East Malham in Craven, Yorkshire, the Property of Lord Ribblesdale)* ?1812–14, exhibited 1815

OVERLEAF Borrowdale and Derwentwater, Cumbria

J.M.W. Turner (1775–1851), *Morning amongst the Coniston Fells,
Cumberland*, exhibited 1798

Based on a tour of the North in 1797,
Turner's picture of Coniston Fells
proclaimed a new art of natural history.

were avid collectors. Classical antiquities and Italian sunshine were now
exchanged, to the patriotic satisfaction of all, for the ancient British landscape and a national architectural heritage. Thomas Girtin's spectacular
Bamburgh Castle (p.23), derived from a tour in 1796, combined both. The
animal painter James Ward found the former at Gordale Scar, a bank of
limestone cliffs near Settle in north Yorkshire. Commisioned by the local
landowner, Lord Ribblesdale, Ward painted what has become the national
masterpiece of the Sublime. Defiant and proud in its immensity, a white
bull watches over cattle and deer and guards the gloomy cataract, which, as
one admirer said, must be approached 'with Awe and a kind of Reverential
Expectation'. Ward finished his picture in 1814, as the European wars were

ending, but he had begun it in 1812, the year Turner adapted a blizzard seen near Farnley (even the British weather could be put to good account) for his epic historical landscape *Snow Storm: Hannibal and his Army Crossing the Alps*. Both pictures put Napoleon firmly in his place, celebrating a nature greater than any human power.

Today we take the cult of landscape, and landscape art, for granted – so much so that it can seem to have nothing new to say. We forget how adventurous it was, when painters were taught to regard landscape painting as an imitative art like portraiture, for the twenty-three year old Turner to paint a picture like *Morning amongst the Coniston Fells* of 1798. This, a product of his 1797 tour, proclaimed a new art of natural history. Its dawn effect was no accident; he exhibited the painting with another sunrise, this time breaking over Norham Castle, on the Tweed in Northumberland. Both were elevated by quotations from English poets. Norham cited the lines about the rising sun from 'Summer' in James Thomson's *Seasons* (1726–30), the most popular nature poem of the eighteenth century, while *Coniston* alluded to Adam and Eve's morning hymn to the Creator in John

J.M.W. Turner (1775–1851), *Norham Castle, Sunrise* 1798

Milton's *Paradise Lost* (completed 1665). Turner's Lakeland is prelapsarian, as primitive as Ward's Yorkshire, but his audience would have recognised it as their paradise found – if until recently 'unsuspected', as Gray had described Grasmere. Writers were ahead of artists here. By the time Turner painted Coniston, Jane Austen had finished *Pride and Prejudice* (1813), in which Elizabeth Bennet, promised a Lake tour by her aunt, asks the very question that his picture tries to answer: 'What are men to rocks and mountains?' In the same year, 1798, Wordsworth and Coleridge's first *Lyrical Ballads* appeared. Here the key work was a Welsh subject, *Tintern Abbey*. But its leap from the pictorial Picturesque to the emotional Sublime – so that a waterfall haunts like a passion and a wood becomes 'a feeling and a love' – was soon reflected in Wordsworth's Lakeland poetry. It gives its own answer to Miss Bennet's question: nature schools the mind of man.

HOME AT GRASMERE

William Wordsworth was a Cumbrian, brought up in Cockermouth where his father was agent to the Lowther estate. By 1799 he was, as he titled a new poem, 'Home at Grasmere' – at Dove Cottage in the adjoining hamlet of Town End. He found both more and less here than Gray's paradise. He wanted it to be not only beautiful, but a miniature of the good society, 'Made for itself . . . unity entire'. In fact this poem was abandoned in its intended form (part of a never-to-be-completed work *The Recluse*) as he became disillusioned with his neighbours. But he admired their rootedness to land and place, 'now almost confined to the North of England'. The first Grasmere poems were vernacular and were chosen, as he told the radical politician Charles James Fox, from 'low and rustic life' because 'in that situation . . . men are incorporated with the beautiful and permanent forms of nature'. Their characters display a noble stoicism, or as he retitled his great poem about the leech-gatherer, *Resolution and Independence*.

In fact it was his sister Dorothy, on her walks round the lake, who first spotted the leech-gatherer, as well as the daffodils dancing in the wind that have become part of the best-loved of all English poems (jointly recited by a record 266,000 children on 19 March 2004, the two-hundredth anniversary of its composition). Her Grasmere journal, written only for herself and 'to give Wm pleasure', is full of vivid descriptions. Her brother

Grasmere

I never saw daffodils so beautiful: they grew among the mossy stones, about and about them. Some rested their heads upon these stones as upon a pillow for weariness, and the rest tossed and reeled and danced, and seemed as if they verily laughed with the wind that blew upon them over the lake, they looked so gay, ever glancing, ever changing...

DOROTHY WORDSWORTH, Grasmere, 15 April 1802

Dove Cottage, Grasmere

transformed them, adding his mind to her eye so that the flowers are stored to bring delight when

> They flash upon that inward eye
> Which is the bliss of solitude.

Memory was vital to Wordsworth's poetic synthesis, as was reflection. At Grasmere he wrote most of *The Prelude* (1805), the greatest of Romantic

creative autobiographies. Years later, aged seventy-three, he still recalled the times and places described in his first account of Lakeland scenery, his student publication *An Evening Walk* (1793), but freed from 'chains of fact and real circumstance'. He had come to Grasmere not only to look about him, but to ask the great questions. *The Recluse*, he told Beaumont in 1804, would contain his 'most interesting feelings concerning Man, Nature, and Society'. These reached far beyond the vale or village that inspired them. In this philosophic mode his mentor was Samuel Taylor Coleridge, also the source of his introduction to Beaumont and his companion at Grasmere on and off between 1800 and 1804.

Coleridge was living at Greta Hall. 'The room in which I write', he told Josiah Wedgwood in November 1800, 'commands six distinct landscapes – the two lakes, the vale, the river, and mountains and mists, and clouds, and sunshine make endless combinations, as if heaven and sky were for ever talking to each other'. Only in the belief in something '*great, one* and indivisible' could 'rocks and waterfalls, mists or caverns, give me the sense of sublimity or majesty'. In 1799 he had described such a transcendent revelation precisely, as he watched the waters of the Greta breaking over a stone and constantly repeating a rose-like pattern: 'still obstinate in resurrection ... *blossoming* in a moment into full flower ... It *is the life* that we live.' Coleridge hardly needed to develop the marvellous descriptions in his notebooks and letters into poetry. His intense looking, his experience of walking and climbing, his faith and his thought were at least a match for Wordsworth's. One thinks of them meeting on their respective walks, at the 'Rock of Names' half-way between their houses, near Wythburn, east of Thirlmere, where they scratched their signatures. Otherwise Coleridge walked by himself. 'Of course it was to me a mere walk', he noted after accompanying Robert Southey and William Hazlitt through Borrowdale in 1803: 'for I must be alone, if either my imagination or heart are to be excited or enriched ... Yet even so I worshipped with deep feeling the grand outline and perpetual Forms ... yea, the very soul of Keswick.'

THE VIEW FROM HELVELLYN

It is as such a worshipper, poised between earth and heaven, that Benjamin Robert Haydon painted his friend Wordsworth in 1843. Wordsworth had already addressed a flattering sonnet to Haydon – 'High is our calling, Friend! – Creative Art'. Now Haydon, who liked to paint great men 'musing' in significant situations – Napoleon on St Helena, Wellington at Waterloo – repaid the compliment with his picture of Wordsworth on Helvellyn. It is Wordsworth as John Keats described him in his sonnet about Haydon, Wordsworth and the journalist Leigh Hunt:

... man was not made to live in great cities ... The pleasures which we receive from rural beauties are of little consequence compared with the moral effect of these pleasures: beholding constantly the best possible, we at last become ourselves the best ...
SAMUEL TAYLOR COLERIDGE, 1795

...like virtue have the forms
Perennial of the ancient hills;
                   nor less
The changeful language of
         their countenances
Quickens the slumbering mind,
      and aids the thoughts
However multitudinous,
               to move
With order and relation.

WILLIAM WORDSWORTH,
The Prelude, 1805

Benjamin Robert Haydon (1786–1846), *William Wordsworth* 1842

Great Spirits now on Earth are sojourning
He of the Cloud, the Cataract, the Lake
Who on Helvellyn's summit wide awake
Catches his freshness from Archangel's wing

Helvellyn was well chosen, for just as Wordsworth presides over these prospects of nature, so the mountain, his alter ego, rules important passages of *The Prelude*, as when 'conscious of the stir' it looks down on the contented bustle of Grasmere fair. Haydon's portrait fixed Wordsworth forever where he belonged.

The poet often climbed Helvellyn, and, ever possessive of it, led Walter Scott and the chemist Humphry Davy to the spot where the body of the young artist Charles Gough was found, after a fall from the mountain in 1805. A Claude glass was in Gough's pocket, but he too had not been satisfied with the distant prospect. A visitor from Manchester, he was a fisherman and a climber as well as a painter. His contemporary claim to fame – reflected in numerous pictures, poems and books – was that his dog was found alive beside his body, whose bones were picked clean of flesh. Was his faithful companion guarding his remains? Or was the dog responsible? The artist Simon Morley has recently reviewed the evidence in a book that is itself a work of art. But today Gough's story is not just a period melodrama, bent as he was on adventure as well as art. There is, said Coleridge in 1802, fresh from climbing Scafell, a sort of gambling; you start down a mountain, with no way of knowing whether your chosen path will continue or end in a precipice, or whether if the latter you will be able to retrace your way – this too might be the life we live.

Thus the Romantics left the Picturesque behind. 'What is a mountain else but a great flat picture . . . placed by Nature on an easel?' Coleridge asked in 1804. He wrote as a climber, and as one who must possess the natural world mentally and imaginatively too, as all Romantics must. But they were privileged pioneers. Coleridge found himself on Scafell in the tracks of a shepherd who had struggled up to rescue a strayed sheep – a reminder that he was himself a man of leisure. Dedicating *The Excursion* to the Earl of Lonsdale in 1814, Wordsworth was grateful to have wandered freely 'through thy fair domains', his right as the agent's son. Across the

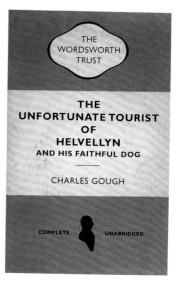

The Unfortunate Tourist of Helvellyn, a book produced by the artist Simon Morley

The view from Helvellyn

Pennines at Haworth in Yorkshire, the young Brontës were free to walk wherever they liked on the moors, because they were children of the parsonage. In 1850 Charlotte wrote that Emily 'found in the bleak solitude many and dear delights; and not the least and best-loved was liberty'. It is easy to see how the windswept wilderness fed the passionate emotions of their novels. Introducing his poem *Michael* (1800), the tale of a Lakeland 'statesman' faced with dispossession of his land, Wordsworth might almost be prefacing *Wuthering Heights* (1847). It was Nature that

> Led me on to feel
> For passions that were not my own, and think
> (At random and imperfectly indeed)
> On man, the heart of man, and human life.

IN AND OUT OF THE LANDSCAPE

Always we must ask – who is a landscape for? Wordsworth gave his own guide to the Lake District (1810, 1822) the distinctly ambiguous conclusion that 'persons of pure taste' had established the district as a 'national property, in which every man has a right and interest who has an eye to perceive and a heart to enjoy'. But Wordsworth, the self-styled 'recluse', and Coleridge, the solitary walker, saw community as well as beauty. Humphry Davy told Coleridge that Wordsworth's *Michael* was 'full of just pictures of what human life ought to be'. Coleridge's own creative autobiography, the *Biographia Literaria* (1817), contrasted the independence and religion of the Lakeland shepherd-farmers with the more degraded peasants of the South. He compared the Lakelanders to the Swiss, also a people of 'mountaineers', and was 'convinced, that for the human soul to prosper in rustic life a certain vantage-ground is prerequisite'. Without it, 'the ancient mountains, with all their terrors and all their glories, are pictures to the blind, and music to the deaf'. This 'natural' order was fragile indeed. Michael's son goes to London – and to the bad. Movement from city to country could be just as destructive. Wordsworth spent his later years fulminating against mass tourism. Campaigning to halt an extension of the Kendal and Windermere railway, he called on 'Mountains, Vales and Floods' to 'Share the passion of a just disdain'.

Haworth Moor, North Yorkshire

One who certainly shared this disdain was Wordsworth's disciple, the writer and art critic John Ruskin, from his retreat at Brantwood, the house overlooking Coniston Water where he moved in 1871. Ruskin loathed the 'Manchester' crush overrunning Keswick, yet made an exception for incomers like himself, nature having given her 'sublime bits' to cultivate 'the highest faculties of perception and feeling'. Brantwood was a private Arcadia in which to dream of the social utopia that he projected over the hills to the working classes in the cities – who were not expected to visit en masse but to receive his wisdom from his publications and educational programmes like those established in Sheffield by his Guild of St George. No new school of Lakeland painters grew up around him. Reversing Coleridge's hymn to the 'mountaineers', Ruskin eventually became convinced that the cruelties of mountain nature killed the souls of those who lived in their shadow. He held that 'mountain truth' was attainable to non-climbers and was contemptuous of those who climbed for sport or dared to claim that their enthusiasm helped them to understand mountains. How it must have hurt him to see the mountains of Cumbria succumbing to the fate of the Alps – 'soaped poles in a bear garden'.

Wordsworth and Ruskin were angry old men. One might make a joke of it, as Dora Carrington did when, lodging in the farm at Watendlath that she painted in 1921, she christened a stuffed stag's head looking super-ciliously down from the wall 'Mr Wordsworth'. Or one might be angry oneself. Growing up on the 'wrong side' of the mountains at Cleator Moor in the bleak 1940s, Conrad Atkinson felt only exclusion from Wordsworth's lakes and their (as they seemed to him) genteel admirers. His ironic work *For Wordsworth; For West Cumbria* juxtaposes Wordsworthian daffodils

... a north-midland shire, dark with moorland, ridged with mountain, this I see. There are great moors behind and on each hand of me; there are waves of mountains far beyond that deep valley at my feet. The population here must be thin, and I see no passengers on these roads ... they are all cut in the moor, and the heather grows deep and wild to their very verge ... I have no relative but the universal mother, Nature: I will seek her breast and ask repose.
CHARLOTTE BRONTË, *Jane Eyre*, 1847

with striking miners whose community was at breaking point. Yet it also reclaims the poet's early radicalism by asking the same question he had asked the leech-gatherer: 'How is it that you live, and what is it that you do?' From the Olympus of Bloomsbury or the desert of a workless town, Wordsworth's vision of rural harmony may indeed seem fatuous. But nor did his 'just disdain' deter the twenty-three year old Alfred Wainwright from hearing the call of the mountains from his native Blackburn. His Lakeland trails, climbs and fell guides with their meticulous maps and drawings and his BBC television films would, he believed, make him as remembered as Wordsworth. He made the landscape his own – for a mass audience. What would Ruskin have thought of Wainwright? Or of William Heaton Cooper, climber-artist and shameless populist whose studio-gallery in Grasmere sold almost 90,000 prints and postcards of his work a year, sending his own picture of Britain around the world. His son Julian's mountain paintings (see p.30), are less topographical and more austere. They are painted from a climber's experience of feel and grip, but also from a rediscovery of Romanticism as a living force. They aim to reconnect us with nature and the landscape, a link that the artist feels has been lost.

Fortunately Ruskin's Coniston, that land of lost content, has also been reclaimed. More positive forces have spread far beyond the lake to dispel

Dora Carrington (1893–1932), *Farm at Watendlath* 1921

Conrad Atkinson (born 1940), *For Wordsworth; for West Cumbria* 1980

Conrad Atkinson felt only exclusion from Wordsworth's lakes and their genteel admirers. His ironic work *For Wordsworth; For West Cumbria* juxtaposes Wordsworthian Nature (daffodils included) with images of a strike-bound mining community.

the gloom of the old prophet's sick mind. From the 1830s until 1894, the Friendly Societies of the Northern cities organised an annual Whitsunday Walk from Coniston for workers, providing them with the air and exercise denied them in their mills and factories. Cooped up for so much of their lives, they laid their limited claim to the wild as a moral right. The mass trespass on the mountain plateau of Kinder Scout in the Derbyshire Peak in 1932, with its pitched battles between ramblers and gamekeepers, was more overtly political. But both events, in their way, contributed to the establishment of the Lake and Peak Districts as the first National Parks in 1951. Meanwhile, the Leeds-born, Rugby School-educated Arthur Ransome, who witnessed the Russian Revolution and married Trotsky's secretary, had not been one to be told what to do or where to keep out. For the plucky child-heroes of his *Swallows and Amazons* (1930) – based on family holidays – Coniston is a glorious adventure-playground in which to learn the lessons of life. Unlike Beatrix Potter's animal characters in her tales set around her Lakeland farm at Sawrey, who stray at their peril and remind us of the disciplines of home and hearth, his children throw themselves open to experience, consumers as well as admirers and students of nature.

Today there is a memorial museum to Potter at Hawkshead, where Wordsworth went to school when not running loose on Lowther land like a 'naked savage'. Wordsworth's own Dove Cottage is now a Centre for British Romanticism. As we have followed the Romantics from pictures and prospects into the landscape – twelve million of us a year to the Lake

District alone – so we have moved on from fireside philosophising and adventures with poets, novelists or self-appointed sages as our guides. We do not forget the cultural memories that have created the demands we make on our landscape. But those memories too, perhaps, are such that our demands can never be fully met. As I write, ramblers have been celebrating the implementation of the Countryside and Rights of Way Act (2000) with a symbolic walk in the Brontës' footsteps starting at the car park at Haworth Parsonage. At the same time, a poll commissioned by the National Trust shows our regret that children can no longer explore the wild alone. We feel this is our legacy, even if it was once exceptional and is now rare. I say 'we'. But the ethnic diversity of today's Britain has been so little represented on guided discovery walks in the Lake District as to call their funding into question, while the photographer Ingrid Pollard, echoing historical apprehensions, has spoken of her 'unease; dread' in the landscape, such that she feels more comfortable with a baseball bat, and observed: 'It's as if the black experience is only lived within an urban environment.' Yet she 'thought she liked the Lake District; where I wandered lonely as a black face in a sea of white'. Pollard acknowledges and subverts cultural stereotypes to make her point. More recently Henna Nadeem has assimilated such classic scenery into her own culture, cutting and inlaying photographs into the organic patterns of Islamic tiles. Surely the depiction and understanding of our landscape have not yet reached the end of their history, as our changing communities discover it afresh.

Ramblers setting out from Haworth Parsonage, summer 2004

When we first meet Charlotte Brontë's Jane Eyre, she is reading Thomas Bewick's *History of British Birds* (1797–1804). Seafowl and their wild haunts have gripped her mind. It is a remarkable projection of a child's imagination into the living natural world, as well as of emotional liberty. For another Yorkshire writer, J.B. Priestley, freedom lay closer, on the moors that, as he tells in his novel *Bright Day* (1946), were a tuppenny bus fare away from Bradford's mills. That closeness of city and wilderness is special to the North. Bewick made and illustrated his wonderful natural history books, *A General History of Quadrupeds* (1790) and *British Birds*, in Newcastle. But he had been brought up on a Northumberland farm and kept both his love of nature and an unsentimental view of country people, who in his brilliant '*tale*-pieces' as he called them are no better than their animals, or actually worse – tying pans to dogs' tails to tease them. Animals were for Bewick the truly legitimate figures in the landscape. When Turner came to the Tyne it was human energy, the coal heavers working during the night loading the Shields colliers, whose terrible beauty captured his imagination. He went on to contrast it to the decadent languor of Venice, already a fallen empire.

Today decay and regeneration are watchwords whenever the city is discussed. Cultural revival, local heritage and new creative communities

J.M.W. Turner (1775–1851), *Shields, on the River Tyne* 1823

L.S. Lowry's landscape is a composite view of industry around Manchester. The Stockport Viaduct appears in the left distance.

L.S. Lowry (1887–1976), *Industrial Landscape* 1955

offset industrial decline, along with the beauty of surrounding country-side. For the Romantics, material destruction lay in the future, but appeared a historical inevitability. Wordsworth thought it only deserved, a punishment for selling our souls. His *Excursion* visits the industrial city – a hell compounded of many northern towns but above all based on Manchester. This is echoed in the sort of composite that L.S. Lowry painted a century later as an existential wasteland or George Orwell described festering in unplanned chaos. It is both the perversion of nature that offends – the brook converted to 'an instrument of deadly bane' to power the looms – and the destruction of community, as entire families are sucked into mines and mills. Coleridge called the mill town 'a Sodom and Gomorrah manu-factory'. Everything becomes a parody, chimneys aping the trees of a forest, bells summoning workers to the factory rather than the congregation to church. The city consumes both life and nature. The extent of its demands is shown, albeit heroically, in Benjamin Williams Leader's extraordinary picture of the excavations for the Manchester Ship Canal. The great work opened in 1894, the same year that the city finished swallowing the little lake of Thirlmere, so idyllically painted by John Glover early in the century, in a larger reservoir.

Ruskin was among the pundits who bemoaned this crime against nature. Manchester argued its right to direct 'this watershed to the purposes of civilisation'. Was physical health less worthy than the spiritual boon that Wordsworth had drawn from nature? In their prime, what often seemed horrific from outside the cities and towns could be a matter of pride within. Their industries and technologies helped form the language of modernism, so often inimical to Romantic naturalism. As master of Newcastle's Government School of Design, William Bell Scott thought Ruskin 'criminal' for teaching students in the Working Men's College to draw stones and moss instead of figures or the useful objects the city made. Shown Halifax by the Yorkshire-born artist Edward Wadsworth, Wyndham Lewis recalled: 'I could see he was proud of it. "It's like Hell, isn't it?" he said enthusiastically.'

The opposition between the country and the city created by the Industrial Revolution is perhaps the reason why the classic view of the industrial city is one observed from without. It is not necessarily disapproving, but it does differentiate. In her novel *North and South* (1855), Mrs Gaskell shows a Hampshire clergyman's daughter overcoming her disdain to appreciate the distinctive values of a cotton-spinning city – which, as

Benjamin Williams Leader (1831–1923), *The Excavation of the Manchester Ship Canal: Eastham Cutting, with Mount Manisty in the Distance* 1891

James Durden's *Summer in Cumberland* is a view of Derwentwater from his house under the mountain Skiddaw.

James Durden (1878–1964), *Summer in Cumberland* 1925

the wife of a Unitarian minister in Manchester, the author knew very well. In *Coronation Street*'s recent New Year's Eve episode Danny Baldwin, the Cockney import to ITV's soap opera, took his reluctant wife to the roof of his factory to admire the 'inspiring' panorama of terraces, chimneys, trams and twinkling lights; he wanted her (and us) to 'see it and share it with him'. William Coldstream and Graham Bell were less enthusiastic when they retreated to the roof of Bolton Art Gallery to paint the smoky townscape in 1938 for the Mass Observation social survey. They might have reflected that northern civic values had long included the arts. Pre-Raphaelitism, with its equal emphasis on truth to nature and moral human tales, found its greatest patrons in the industrial North. Manchester became a consumer not only of Lake District water, but, through its art gallery, of pictures of Lakeland scenery, like James Durden's *Summer in Cumberland* (1925) – Arcadia with afternoon tea, a dream that haunts us still. Royle's view of the steel metropolis of Sheffield (p.29), meanwhile, has passed into history, and the city's latest draw is an indoor garden. Perhaps Ivor Gatty, art critic of the *Yorkshire Post*, tempted providence too far when he wrote in 1923, praising the 'sublimity' of the scene, that 'here are forged the tools by which man's greatest conquests over nature have been won'.

The Home Front

"Thank goodness for the sea, our protector. When I swam as a child at Hastings I used to wonder whether the water I was touching was the same water that Julius Caesar had touched when he invaded Britain."

The South East has been punished for its proximity to the nation's capital. Today it is a sprawl of new executive homes (developer-speak for houses just a little smaller, less well placed and altogether less desirable than the glossy brochures advertising them suggest) and their satellites: shopping malls, multi-storey car parks, leisure centres, and by-passes with their sodium lights piercing the night sky and obliterating the stars. But even today beneath the carapace it is possible to find traces of what the South East once was.

Two hundred years ago it contained some of the finest countryside in Britain and was used as London's lungs, an escape from the squalor, stench and noise of the city. William Blake moved to the south coast in 1803. He lived in a cottage, which still stands, overlooking a cornfield that led to the beach. Today of course houses block the view, but then he wrote of Felpham as 'a sweet place for study because it is more spiritual than London'. In 1827 the painter Samuel Palmer followed Blake to his own 'little village safe and still, where

pain and vice full seldom come': Shoreham in Kent, a county now split in half by roads to the Channel Tunnel and high-speed rail links. But explore Kent to the east, beyond the last motorway, and you can still enter a lost world of quiet villages punctuated by their church spires: the world Blake and Palmer knew. Or go up behind Felpham, onto the Downs at Goodwood, and stride the soft turf Blake knew and enjoy majestic views across the English Channel.

Thank goodness for the sea, our protector. When I swam as a child at Hastings I used to wonder whether the water I was touching was the same water that Julius Caesar had touched when he invaded Britain. Scientifically dubious, maybe, but it contains a germ of truth. This sea we watch today, its tides and winds creating their typical steep short waves with curling crests is, like the sky, the one sight we can be sure Julius Caesar did see, and William the Conqueror for that matter. It is also a view that Napoleon and Hitler would have loved to see from our side of the Channel. It is Shakespeare's 'silver sea

The Needles, Isle of Wight

... as a moat defensive to a house against the envy of less happier lands' and Turner's tumultuous seas, showing man's struggle against nature but also Britain's struggle against her enemies.

I took my own boat, a half-decked gaff-rigged cutter, to sail the sea Turner painted. *Rocket* was built in Falmouth along the lines of the many thousands of small boats that fished or traded around our shores a hundred years ago. She is designed to be heavy and powerful and to keep going through the waves. We went out to the Needles off the Isle of Wight, and through the Hurst narrows past the forts built in Tudor times to protect the entrance to our main defensive naval harbour at Portsmouth, sailing over a graveyard of more than two thousand ships. The weather was benign as it was in some of Turner's later, and rather unexpected, paintings of regatta sailing at Cowes when the wars with France were over and peaceful pursuits could be taken up once more.

War and peace: the dominant images of a South East still littered with fortresses, Martello Towers, anti-tank emplacements. It is not surprising that this coastline has come to symbolise Britain's defiance of so many threats. The White Cliffs themselves seem to stand for the

Churchill's home at Chartwell

indomitable spirit we pride ourselves on and have been used as propaganda long before Vera Lynn sang 'There'll be bluebirds over the White Cliffs of Dover'. It is churlish to point out that the White Cliffs are no defence at all, since they are regularly broken up by the wide and gently sloping beaches which made a perfect landing spot for William in 1066. It is the unpredictable ferocity of the Channel which has been our main defence.

During the Battle of Britain in 1940 the south-east corner of Kent, where young fighter pilots duelled for control of the skies, was nicknamed Hellfire Corner. Paul Nash's paintings vividly recorded the scene. Near here is the old home of Winston Churchill at Chartwell. It is not too fanciful to think that when he stayed here, out of office, brooding over the way Britain was sliding into war, he looked out over the landscape beyond his house and saw in it an image of the Britain he wanted to save. It is spectacular but of an entirely domestic and well-tended beauty. Some of the pictures in his studio,

which are not among his best works, show how he responded to it.

Churchill was an amateur painter. In his years in the political wilderness he described how 'the muse of painting came to my rescue . . . and said "are these toys any good to you? They amuse some people"'. His output was prodigious and energetic. He took lessons from professional painters who were friends and developed his own style marked by dramatic use of light and shade and strong colours. No-one, least of all himself, would have compared him with the great

Seven Sisters chalk cliffs between Seaford and Eastbourne

painters that hang on the walls of our art galleries and museums. But he is worth a second look because he stands as a fine example of the long and enduring tradition of amateur artists in Britain which dates back to the seventeenth century. Amateur painters in oil, or more often in watercolour are part of our artistic heritage. They train their eyes to see and interpret. If the results are less skilled than the professional artist's they are nonetheless part of our landscape culture, people who try to see and interpret nature for themselves, and reap the benefits of their study. I know what I am talking about because I draw when I can and learn from the act of drawing. I only show what I have done to my family and they would never qualify for the walls of a gallery. But that is not the point. It is the act of putting pencil, pen or brush to paper that matters. Perhaps, if you never have, Churchill's example will encourage you, where Turner's example may scare you witless.

OVERLEAF
Frank Newbould (1887–1951),
Your Britain, Fight for it Now
(*The South Downs*) 1942 (detail)

War and Peace

CHRISTINE RIDING

When Britain first at heaven's command,
Arose from out the azure main,
This was the charter of the land,
And guardian angels sung this strain:

'Rule Britannia, rule the waves,
Britons never shall be slaves'.

These famous words were written in 1740 and originally formed part of a masque celebrating Alfred the Great, who had defended Anglo-Saxon England from Viking invasion and is claimed to be the father of the English navy. Performed only thirty-three years after the Act of Union between Scotland, Wales and England, the song quickly became a patriotic anthem and the first to celebrate 'Britain'. But what exactly did it celebrate? Firstly, that Britain was an island nation. Secondly, that Britain was a maritime nation with imperial ambitions. Thirdly, that Britons were unconquerable. Thus the bond between Britons was described in terms of the geographical boundary afforded by the coast, where land and sea meet, which defined, unified and protected the population within, and acted as a physical and psychological barrier to the enemy without.

As the historian Linda Colley has noted, Britain was 'an invention forged above all by war.' The Acts of Union (1707 and 1800) were designed to prevent French invasions of England and Wales being launched from Scotland and Ireland. Of course, chiefly thanks to its geography, the British Isles had not experienced a successful invasion since the Norman Conquest of 1066. The inhospitable seas around Scotland and Ireland had destroyed the mighty Spanish Armada in 1588, following the fleet's inconclusive engagement with the English navy off the south coast. But the invasion threat remained, above all in the vulnerable south-eastern coast of England, being the closest to the Continent. Its position as the first line of defence is demonstrated by the accumulation over centuries of fortified ports and defences, such as the Cinq Ports of Kent and East Sussex, Dover Castle, the Martello towers (1804–8), and Second World War 'pill-boxes'. But if the sea proved a natural defence, it was often perilous to the numerous Britons who travelled upon it and gained employment by it. In the introduction to his popular publication

Paul Nash (1889–1946),
The Battle of Britain 1941 (detail)

Shipwrecks and Disasters at Sea (1812) John Graham Dalyell noted that 'every individual is either immediately or remotely connected to the fortune of the sea'. From the sixteenth century, British ships had begun to cover the globe, exploring, trading, colonising or fighting. The naval victories of the Nile (1795), Trafalgar (1805) and St Domingo (1806) established British maritime supremacy, the perception that the Royal Navy was invincible and spawned a national hero, Horatio Nelson. But if the British now controlled what happened on the waves, ruling the waves was much more problematic. Seafaring was a dangerous occupation, especially around the British coastline, and shipwreck was greatly feared and often experienced. Dalyell calculated that 5,000 Britons perished at sea every year. Perhaps not surprisingly, 'storm at sea' and 'shipwreck' were major themes in art, literature, theatre and popular entertainments and became metaphors for social and political upheaval, featuring in numerous satirical prints by James Gillray and others. In this context, J.M.W. Turner's *The Shipwreck*, painted during the Napoleonic War, would have been appreciated on various levels, not simply as a *tour de force* in capturing the sublime power of the elements. But the exposure to danger at sea was given a patriotic spin, because, as one commentator noted, it 'materially contributes to the formation of [national] character'. Thus British sailors, fortified by courage and endurance, 'are invariably the first in matters of

J.M.W. Turner (1775–1851), *The Shipwreck* exhibited 1805

From the beginning of the French Revolutionary war in 1793, there was a constant fear of invasion of England or Ireland. This is the first of many prints by Gillray on the subject, which are often deliberately crude underlining the terror felt by many at the idea of the French succeeding.

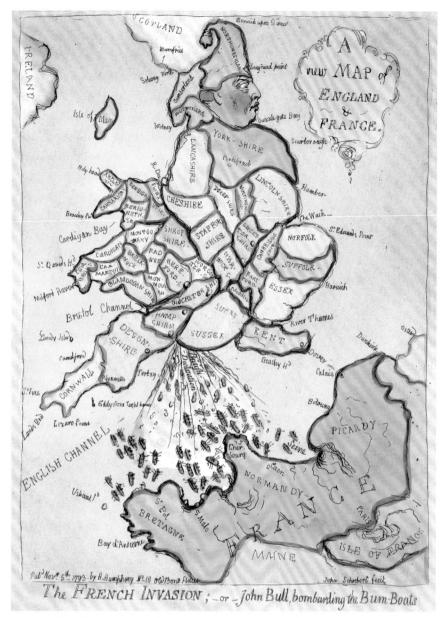

James Gillray (1757–1815), *The French Invasion; – or – John Bull, bombarding the Bum-Boats* 1793

the most daring enterprise'. The notion of stoical determination and resilience as characteristics of the British island race is the subject of Gillray's *The French Invasion; – or – John Bull, bombarding the Bum-Boats* (November 1793). King George III, in the guise of the map of Britain, goes to war, crapping gun boats onto the coast of France, a crude, no-nonsense action, depicted by Gillray as heroic, patriotic and contemptuous.

But 'islandness' was not created by a burgeoning British national identity. It had been part of English national consciousness for centuries. In Shakespeare's *Richard II* (1597) John of Gaunt famously describes the English – 'This happy breed of men' – as the product of England itself,

William Powell Frith (1819–1909), *The Derby Day* 1856–8

'this sceptred isle... this precious stone set in a silver sea'. This speech –
often misrepresented as a piece of unadulterated patriotism – is a bitter
remonstrance against the evils of misrule and what could be lost as a result.
Shakespeare was writing at a time of national crisis surrounding the
succession to the throne, which saw the rebellion (albeit ill-fated) led
by the Earl of Essex against the ageing Elizabeth I (1601). The natural
bond between the land and the people is perhaps an obvious analogy for
Shakespeare to have made in pre-industrial Elizabethan England. But, as
Alex Potts and Jane Beckett have noted (in reference to the late nineteenth
century), characterising 'the English countryside as the essence of Englishness' was 'a defence mechanism, incorporated and mobilised as a national
mythology in times of political and national tension'. This is especially
true during times of war. The vision of the English landscape – especially
in relation to the South – that was returned to again and again, was
that described in Shakespeare's celebrated eulogy, 'This other Eden,
demi-paradise . . . This blessed plot, this earth, this realm, this England.'

It was a vision influenced by the rise of tourism from the eighteenth
century. The southern counties and coastline were not only the first line
of defence, above all for the capital, London, but increasingly the playground of the metropolis. *The Derby Day* (1856–8) by William Powell Frith
shows a panorama of Victorian urban society gathered for a day out in
Epsom, Surrey. As the artist J.E. Hodgson noted, 'The races of Epsom Downs,
the great Saturnalia of British sport, brings to the surface all that is most
characteristic of London life. In this picture we discern its elements, its

luxury, its wealth, its beauty, its refinement, its hopeless misery'. The coast itself became increasingly the site of recreation rather than defence, giving rise to the modern culture of tourism. But this focus on leisure and the English landscape and coastal areas was encouraged by war. Cowes Regatta, for example, hosted by the Royal Yachting Club at Cowes on the Isle of Wight, originated from the Napoleonic War period when travelling to the continent was all but impossible. Eventually the regatta was given the royal seal of approval by King George IV and was held on an annual basis from 1826. From this point onwards, it rapidly became a fixture in London's society calendar and a subject for painters including Turner in 1827 and James Tissot and Philip Wilson Steer later in the century. In *A Procession of Yachts*, begun at Cowes in 1892, Steer represents this quintessentially English leisure activity using the cutting-edge technical and compositional practices of French artists such as Seurat and Pissarro.

The seaside resort was invented during the eighteenth century and popularised by 1900. In 1730, the wealthy had begun to visit the coast for health reasons. As the century progressed, numbers and expectations rose and coastal towns, in particular Brighton, were developed to include facilities available in London and the fashionable spa town of Bath. By the time John Constable took his wife, Maria, to Brighton in 1824 to restore her health, a good coach service existed from London, John Nash had recently completed the exotic Royal Pavilion for George IV (1815–23), and the Chain Pier (1823) and the York, the first of the large hotels (1819), had been built. 'Brighton', Constable wrote, 'is the receptacle of the

OVERLEAF The South Downs   Philip Wilson Steer (1860–1942), *A Procession of Yachts* 1892–3

John Constable (1776–1837), *Chain Pier, Brighton* 1826–7

fashion and offscouring of London. The magnificence of the sea, and its. . . everlasting voice, is drowned in the din & lost in the tumult of stage coaches – gigs – 'flys' &c. – and the beach is only piccadilly . . . by the sea-side.' The conflation of fishing town and fashionable resort was captured by the artist in *Chain Pier, Brighton*, exhibited at the Royal Academy in 1827, showing the Albion Hotel and pump-room (far left), the Marine Parade and Chain Pier, bathing huts, fishermen and sightseers walking along the beach.

By the 1830s Brighton was the most popular seaside resort in Britain, accommodating approximately 2,000 visitors a week. Nationally speaking, visitor numbers accelerated during the Victorian period with the opening of railway links from London to Brighton (1841), Eastbourne (1849) and so on. Cornwall was the last English county to be connected to a railway network, in 1859. The railway company in charge of the London–Brighton route initially concentrated on first-class travellers but soon realised that reducing third-class tickets would increase the number of customers. This was done in 1843 and in the next six months 360,000 passengers travelled to Brighton. The development of Cornwall as a major tourist destination after 1900 was largely led by promotions such as the Great Western Railway's successful marketing campaign of 'the Cornish Riviera'. By 1911, an estimated fifty-five per cent of the population of England and Wales made at least one seaside trip per year: the 'bucket and spade' holiday had arrived. The appeal of the coast (and the countryside in general) was partly as an escape from the city. As Norman Garstin wrote in *The Studio* (1909), 'To those who live in the crowded centres the very thought of capes and headlands which thrust themselves out into the lonely sea comes with a

William Dyce (1806–1864), *Pegwell Bay, Kent – a Recollection of October 5th 1858* ?1858–60

sense of relief from the jostle and jumble of the intricate schemes of city life.' William Dyce's *Pegwell Bay, Kent* (?1858–60) was painted after a holiday trip in October 1858. People are engaged in undemanding, gentle pursuits, gathering shells and exploring rock pools, a popular pastime from mid-century onwards. And 'people at leisure', as a way of picturing modern life (as opposed to industry) was a favourite theme of later artists who took advantage of new travel opportunities. Steer often visited friends at Walberswick, Suffolk, and produced a number of works that were not only modern in subject (that is picturing leisure and tourism) but some of the most technically advanced Impressionist works produced in Britain, an example being *The Beach at Walberswick* (?c.1889). But the popularity of the coast also related to more general concerns about the moral and physical health of the nation. Thus walking, sunbathing and taking in the fresh air and views of unadulterated nature were seen as morally and physically beneficial. Henry Tuke's *August Blue* (1893–4), for example, underlines the idea of innocent, healthy recreation, with the archetypes of national youth boating in Falmouth Harbour, Cornwall, bathed in sunlight. But the

Henry Scott Tuke (1858–1929), *August Blue* 1893–4

Philip Wilson Steer (1860–1942), *The Beach at Walberswick* ?c.1889

offshoot of this partial appreciation of the coast, as Ysanne Holt has noted, was that painting was 'affected by greater appreciation of what made the area appealing for the tourist and, by extension, the picture buyer.' Thus artists very rarely produced images of Cornwall's traditional industries, such as tin mining, focusing instead on 'beaches and cliff tops'. And this was equally true of artists painting the coastal communities, in particular those who settled in Newlyn village, such as Stanhope Forbes and Frank Bramley. Between 1880 and 1900, 'fisherfolk' and 'peasants', were the two most popular genre subjects on the walls of the Royal Academy. Whether sentimentalised or not, the paintings sent back to London audiences, such as *A Fish Sale on a Cornish Beach* (1885) by Stanhope Forbes, promoted the notion of a traditional way of life, far removed from the complexities of the modern, urban experience. It was thus a highly selective, essentially city-generated vision, and one that finds parallels in the work of artists a century earlier.

ENGLISHNESS AND THE RURAL IDYLL

William Blake was not a landscape artist, but the rural was an important element in his work. His most famous lines from the prophetic poem *Milton* (1804) – popularly known as 'Jerusalem' – are a commentary on the political, social and spiritual crisis of his time, described as an interrelationship between the English nation, the landscape and Christianity:

> And did those feet in ancient time,
> Walk upon England's mountains green:
> And was the holy Lamb of God,
> On England's pleasant pastures seen!

John Linnell (1792–1882), *Harvest Moon* 1858

And did the Countenance Divine
Shine forth upon our clouded hills,
And was Jerusalem builded here
Among these dark satanic mills?

This emphasis also pervades Blake's work uniting word and image. In *Songs of Innocence* (1789), a series of short lyrical verses and images, the pastoral tone is established from the beginning with the narrator as a shepherd, who, walking through an idyllic woodland setting, receives inspiration from a child in a cloud to pipe his songs celebrating the Divine in nature. Blake's vision of the countryside had very little to do with reality, a retreat not simply from the urban to the rural, but to the landscape of the imagination. This is evident in his unconventional (and subsequently influential) wood-cut illustrations to Thornton's *The Pastorals of Virgil* (1821). In these small-scale works, Blake developed a new kind of pastoral image with landscape presented in purely visionary terms. In *The Blighted Corn* and *Sabrina's Silvery Flood*, trees, rivers, animals, farm buildings and the moon assume an intense, otherworldly appearance.

Samuel Palmer (1805–1881), *Coming from Evening Church* 1830

By the end of his life, Blake was surrounded by a group of acolytes, including the landscape painters Samuel Palmer and John Linnell. Together they formed a group called The Ancients and set up an artists' colony in the village of Shoreham, Kent. There they donned medieval dress, wore their hair long and sported beards. Unlike Blake, who in religious terms was a non-conformist (as well as a political radical), the

Ancients were solidly Anglican. Inspired by the example of Blake's visionary landscape, they attempted to find expressions of their spirituality in the Kent countryside itself: seeking 'the Countenance Divine' in 'England's green and pleasant land'. Palmer's *Coming from Evening Church* represents a peaceful, Christian Arcadia with the village church at the heart of the community. John Linnell's later works, *Harvest Moon*, showing labourers returning from the fields, and *Contemplation*, with a shepherd and his flock, are similarly poetic evocations of the gentle timelessness of rural life, inspired by the Surrey landscape surrounding his home in Redhill. Given this loaded interpretation of the English village and the countryside and the symbolic parallel between the shepherd and his flock and the parish priest and his congregation, it is not surprising that contemporary commentators in 1852 sought biblical meanings in *Our English Coasts, 1952 ('Strayed Sheep')* by William Holman Hunt. Set in an idyllic location overlooking Covehurst Bay near Hastings, this highly detailed, luminous painting shows an unattended flock perilously close to the edge of a cliff.

William Holman Hunt (1827–1910), *Our English Coasts, 1852 ('Strayed Sheep')* 1852

H. Gawthorn (1879–1941), *Women's Land Army (God Speed the Plough and the Woman who Drives It)*, after 1917

Since the Church was traditionally perceived as a unifying force in society, Hunt's painting suggests that its representatives, the clergy, are neglectful of the nation's spiritual welfare, or perhaps the painting symbolises in more general terms contemporary concerns surrounding religious disunity and sectarianism.

Undoubtedly the religious overtones of *Our English Coasts* were intentional. Holman Hunt was fully engaged with the religious debates of his time and believed that art had a moral role in society. But the fact that links were also made between the painting and concerns about foreign invasion underlines the truth that by the mid-nineteenth century there was a commonly held assumption that landscapes and coastal scenes were imbued with significance that went far beyond the representation of a specific location or an artist's singular vision. At the end of the nineteenth century, nostalgia for rural life and anti-urbanism, encouraged by tourism, were paralleled by developing notions of national identity, character and the countryside. For many, English culture was a *country* culture. And by extension, the national character was represented in rural and coastal communities, not in England's industrial cities. *Cook's Traveller Gazette*, for example, identified the Cornish people with the land, which, according to the writer, they had inhabited and tended since time immemorial: 'Here in a tempered climate fanned by healthful breezes flourish a hardy, thrifty and hospitable people. . . tilling the soil once trodden by ancient saints'. And the harsh realities of rural life, for example, ploughing and reaping, as time-honoured, pre-industrial occupations were romanticised, transforming the rural labourer into a cultural icon. Just how resonant this image was can be gleaned by a Government recruitment poster, published in 1917, for the Women's Land Army, showing a female labourer in an idyllic setting (shades of Blake and Palmer?) with the strap line, 'God Speed the Plough and the Woman Who Drives It'. A similar transformation occurred with the English village and by association the country cottage. For many, the village came to represent an unspoilt element of national culture, an ideal habitat, handed down from generation to generation, in perfect harmony with nature. In 1912, an article published in *The Spectator* expressed a widely held view that the village was in danger of disappearing, and suggested that the National Trust (founded in 1895) should purchase an 'ideal hamlet'. Similar views were expounded prior to the Second World War, for example, in broadcasts by the BBC entitled 'The National

Character' (October–December 1933). The writer and presenter of these programmes, Arthur Bryant, published the scripts in *The Listener*. In 1933, he wrote that 'the only lasting Utopia for [every Englishman] must lie in a rose garden and a cottage in the country'.

How did art figure in these debates? Was there such a thing as an English subject or way of painting? And what influence, if any, should contemporary foreign art have? In very general terms 'English' art was categorised as 'traditional', in contrast to 'modern' art, which was perceived as 'French' (as represented by Impressionism). Thus categorised, modern art was, by its very nature, a form of invasion, which to some was only marginally less threatening than a foreign army. By the 1890s, there were numerous commentators of the opinion that the golden age of English art – which displayed an authentic national character – came from the eighteenth and early nineteenth century. In terms of landscape, deemed the most English of painting genres, emphasis was placed on artists of the Romantic period. But although Turner, Thomas Girtin and John Sell Cotman were discussed as quintessentially English landscape artists, it was Constable who was thought fully to embody the English character and aesthetic in art. In 1906, Sir James Linton wrote in the *Magazine of Art*, 'His vigorous treatment of his subjects, his largesse of view and full colour, seems to be typical of the sturdy yeoman of this country of ours ... He loved his England with her rich glowing colours, and all the signs of her prosperity that surrounded him in his native country.' The timing is crucial. By 1900, artists such as Constable and Turner not only represented 'tradition' and 'nature', key words in any contemporary discussion of national art, but also provided reassurance and continuity in an uncertain world, moving inevitably, it would seem, towards war.

The debate over national identity and the Englishness of English art (to borrow Nikolaus Pevsner's phrase) developed and intensified during the first quarter of the twentieth century. This is not surprising during a period marked by the First World War, the Great Depression, the Russian Revolution and the rise of Communism and Fascism. Paul Nash, who was largely unaffected by the Vorticist movement led by Wyndham Lewis, was seen in the 1920s as having proved his national artistic credentials by working in the tradition of Constable and the Romantic watercolourists. But Nash was also influenced by Blake and Palmer. Indeed, their fusion of English landscape with the religious and the visionary also inspired artists such as

John Nash (1893–1977), *The Cornfield* 1918

In 1918, John Nash wrote that he and his brother Paul used to paint for their own pleasure only after six o'clock, when their work as war artists was over for the day. This is shown in the painting by the long shadows cast by the evening sun across the field.

Graham Sutherland and Stanley Spencer. This is particularly evident in Spencer's immortalisation of the Berkshire village of Cookham-on-Thames, which finds parallels with Shoreham and the Ancients. But Spencer went further, imagining biblical events, including Christ's crucifixion, in the streets, lanes and surrounding fields of his home village. Part of the renewed interest in artists like Blake was that they were thought to represent an idiosyncratic English vision and could therefore be utilised by artists like Paul Nash and his brother John in the development of a modern English style. Thus John Nash's *The Cornfield* looks both modern and traditional. But the nostalgic element in these works, post 1918, may be linked to the experience of war. The Nash brothers had been to the Western Front and Spencer had returned from active duty suffering from 'war depression' sensing, in his words, a 'Loss of Eden'. Cookham itself had suffered numerous casualties, including Spencer's brother Sydney. *Resurrection, Cookham* (1824–7), a vast canvas showing bodies rising from their graves in the village churchyard, may in part represent the artist's longing for the community to be made whole again. And when the Nashes returned to England, they rented a studio in Chalfont St Giles, Buckinghamshire, and painted their monumental war commissions, *The Menin Road* and *Over the Top. The Cornfield,* mentioned above, was painted at the same time, a poignant contrast to these panoramas of devastation and death.

THE ART OF DEFENCE

At the turn of the twentieth century, there was a general assumption that
Britannia still ruled the waves, and that the coast continued to be a natural
and (as history had proved) largely inviolate boundary. Thus 'islandness'
was characterised as quintessentially English (if not British) in comment-
aries during the First World War. As the century progressed, however, this
notion was severely tested. From 1914, aeroplanes were used in combat
for the first time, a sign of things to come. And in 1915, Germany launched
the first of a series of raids on England using Zeppelin airships. During
the next two years, many places were affected, along the east coast, in the
Midlands, Home Counties and London's East End, even as far north as
Edinburgh. German war propaganda celebrated these attacks through
posters and postcards, one showing a combined invasion force of battle-
ships and Zeppelins, advancing on the south coast with the strap line,
'Wir Kommen, England!' (We are coming, England!) In fact the fatalities
and damage inflicted during these raids were light, the Zeppelin being
vulnerable to bad weather and the increasing accuracy of British fighter-
pilots and anti-aircraft gunners. But the impact on morale was profound.
For the first time, Britons were faced with the realisation that invasion
could come from the sky. In 1915, *The Times* noted that the nation had lost
'the age old immunity at the heart of the British empire from the sight of
the foe and the sound of an enemy missile'. This message was hammered
home by Government propaganda and recruitment posters. One entitled
'The Hun and the Home' underlined exactly what was in danger by juxta-
posing an idyllic, sunlit village scene ('A Bit of England') with a bombed
out town ('A Bit of Belgium').

The warning of the First World War was to be fulfilled during the
Second (1939–45). Indeed with the Battle of Britain (1940), the Blitz (1940–1)
and the so-called Baedeker raids (1942), war had finally come to mainland
Britain. In 1940, with the retreat of the British Expeditionary Force from
Dunkirk and victorious German troops marching on to Paris, Britain
was isolated. The desperate situation was encapsulated by David Low's
cartoon, published in the *Evening Standard* on 18 June 1940, showing a
British soldier standing on a stormy coastline, defiantly shaking his fist
at the Luftwaffe with the caption, 'Very Well, Alone!' On the same day,
Churchill famously noted, 'the Battle of France is over. I expect that the

Frank Newbould (1887–1951), *Your Britain, Fight for it Now (Salisbury Cathedral)* 1942

Frank Newbould (1887–1951), *Your Britain, Fight for it Now (The South Downs)* 1942

Battle of Britain is about to begin. Upon this battle depends the survival of Christian civilization. Upon it depends our own British life, and the long continuity of our institutions and our Empire.' By November 1940, Hitler's plans to invade Britain had been frustrated by the tenacity of the Royal Air Force and coastal defence and his attention turned to the Soviet Union. However, air raids and invasion scares continued until 1944.

In an art context, the effect of these events was to make redundant the distinction made during the First World War between the 'artists at the front' and the 'artists at home'. In 1918 John Nash noted the superiority felt by the soldier-artists over those artists in Britain painting (to use his phrase) 'the knitting of woolly garments'. This was no longer the case. The experience of war was now on the doorstep. In 1939 the War Artists Advisory Committee was set up, with the then Director of the National Gallery, Kenneth Clark, as the chairman. Official war artists and other artists commissioned by the WAAC included some from the First World War, such as Paul and John Nash and Stanley Spencer, as well as new recruits, Eric Ravilious, John Piper, Graham Sutherland, Henry Moore and many others. As previously discussed, a number of these artists were exploring the traditional and the modern in art (represented in the 1920s and 1930s by abstraction and Surrealism). Thus war commissions by Paul Nash and his pupil and friend Ravilious demonstrate a rural nostalgia as well as a fascination for the modern world. And none of these can be described as documentary artists. Indeed, the project's aim, as described by Clark, was 'to provide a memorable record of the war and its associated activities'. This, he felt, would be best served by the employment of artists, who were 'more sensitive and observant than ordinary people' and the medium of art, which would give permanent expression to 'certain important but fleeting emotions aroused by the war'.

Clearly, the WAAC had a view on what it deemed appropriate subjects and themes in terms of public relations and propaganda. Not surprisingly, images of panic and confusion, carnage, looting and riots were non-existent. Bombing raids on ports and coastal defences were recorded, but at an appropriate distance, as in *Night Raid on Portsmouth Docks* (1941) by Richard Eurich and *Shelling by Night* (1941) by Ravilious. As the author and scholar Stephen Spender wrote, 'The background to this war, corresponding to the Western Front in the last war, is the bombed city.' Indeed, some of the iconic images of the war in Britain involved urban bombing, in particular St Paul's Cathedral framed by the smoke of the Blitz or Churchill standing on the rubble of the House of Commons chamber. Henry Moore's celebrated drawings of people sheltering from air raids in the London Underground, exhibited at the National Gallery in 1941, were often interpreted as metaphors for the stoical resistance shown by the British during wartime. Both John Piper and Graham Sutherland were commissioned to record buildings or streets soon after they were hit by German bombs. During the London Blitz, the worst of the bombing was centred on the East End. Sutherland, who visited the area, thought the ruined streets were

Henry Moore's celebrated drawings of people sheltering from an air raid in the London Underground were often interpreted as metaphors for the stoical resistance shown by the British during wartime.

Henry Moore (1898–1986), *Tube Shelter Perspective* 1941

Thomas Monnington (1902–1976), *Southern England: Spitfires Attacking Flying-Bombs* 1944

'tremendously moving . . . mysterious and sad', sentiments he sought to capture in his paintings. And in the spring of 1942, the Baedeker Blitz was launched in retaliation for the Allied bombing of Lübeck, Cologne and Rostock. The targets were English cities that were strategically un-important but historically significant, essentially rural (in comparison to conurbations like London and Manchester) and aesthetically picturesque, and thus considered by many to be the very essence of England itself. As legend has it, the selection was made using the German Baedeker tourist guide to Britain (the Nazi propagandist, Baron Gustav Braun von Storm allegedly stated, 'We shall go out and bomb every building in Britain marked with three stars'.) Between April and June, Bath, Canterbury, Exeter, Norwich and York were attacked. Commenting on Piper's images of the damage in Bath, John Betjeman noted the wider significance of these targets: 'When the bombs fell, when the city churches crashed, when the classic and Perpendicular glory of England was burnt and stark, he produced a series of oil paintings, using his theory of colour to keep the drama of a newly fallen bomb alive.' The attacks on more rural locations must have given additional poignancy to a series of Government propaganda posters published in the same year. Under the title 'Your Britain, Fight for it Now!' the scenes focus entirely on the countryside and rural life: 'The South Downs', 'Salisbury Cathedral', 'Oak Tree' and 'Alfriston Fair' (see pp.58–9, 78).

WAR IN THE AIR

Arguably the most original and challenging landscapes from this period came in response to aerial warfare. In August 1940, Paul Nash submitted a series of watercolours entitled *Raiders* or *Marching Against England*, each featuring a crashed German fighter plane or bomber in a rural setting, such as the White Cliffs on the southern coast. On one level, these deeply symbolic, patriotic images, as Nash stated, were 'designed to emphasise the incongruity of the alien machines, helpless, out of their element, in the idyllic English landscape'. For Nash, the protagonists of the conflict were not men, but machines. 'This is the War of Machines,' he stated, 'and they have taken on human and animal appearances'. In *Bomber in the Corn*, *The Messerschmidt in Windsor Great Park* and *Under the Cliff* he eschewed factual representation seeking instead to portray the aircraft as if they were living creatures, imbuing them, as the poet and writer Herbert Read noted, 'with an additional mystery, ominous and deathly.' The WAAC members were thrilled with the results. Not so the Air Ministry or the RAF, who as a rule demanded accurate detailing of scenery and especially aircraft, favouring works that promoted the 'gentlemanliness' and heroism of the Fighter Command pilots. Consequently, the RAF employed its own artists on the basis, as Clark concluded, that the WAAC's 'taste [was] too modern'. Commissions continued, however, supplementing those of the RAF. Some of the most resonant in the context of this essay were the aerial combat scenes by Thomas Monnington, *Southern England, 1944: Spitfires Attacking Flying-Bombs* and *Southern England, 1944: Tempests Attacking Flying-Bombs* (both 1944). Towards the end of the war, the infamous V1 (also known as the 'flying bomb' or 'doodlebug') was used to attack targets in south-eastern England. Initially the only successful defence was interception by a small group of high-performance fighter planes, including the Spitfire and the newly developed Hawker Tempest. Monnington shows the fighter planes pursuing the V1 bombs along an idyllic rural vista or above a group of oast houses in Kent. Significantly, given the adulation surrounding Constable as the painter of the quintessential English landscape, the foregrounds include details of a cart and a jumping horse reminiscent of *The Hay Wain* (1819) and *The Leaping Horse* (1825).

If the RAF found Nash and others interpretations too 'modern', there was no denying their patriotic intent. Nash supported the use of art as

Paul Nash (1889–1946), *Totes Meer (Dead Sea)* 1940–1

propaganda and sought, through images of the defeated enemy, 'to strike a blow on behalf of the RAF, apart from any triumph of art for its own sake'. This is evident in *Totes Meer (Dead Sea)*, perhaps the most celebrated British painting of the war, which Nash thought 'would make a good reproduction for depressing the Nazis'. The painting was worked up from sketches and photographs of crashed German aeroplanes in a dump at Cowley outside Oxford. Albeit based on an actual scene, Nash's landscape is an eerie one, formed by 'hundreds and hundreds of flying creatures which invaded these shores'. Clearly the incursion of enemy fighter planes gave British artists a unique opportunity to create a new kind of symbolic landscape art. This is especially true of artistic representations of aerial combat over the English landscape, above all during the Battle of Britain when some inhabitants of the southern counties witnessed the fighting happening overhead. Nash's next major work took this crucial battle as its theme. As with *Totes Meer*, he produced an imaginative rather than literal representation, 'an attempt', he said, 'to give the *sense* of an aerial battle in operation over a wide area and thus summarise England's

Paul Nash (1889–1946), *The Battle of Britain* 1941

great aerial victory over Germany'. In contrast, Richard Eurich painted a panoramic scene on the same subject entitled *Air Fight over Portland* (1940) showing an actual event with an accurate depiction of the harbour in Dorset, with Sandfoot Castle, one of Henry VIII's coastal defences, in the foreground. Thus Eurich's work gives a much clearer impression than Nash's of how the battle might have appeared to spectators on the ground. Nash, however, was attempting something less specific and palpable. In *Battle of Britain*, he draws out the strange, otherworldliness of the scene, above all with the swirling pattern of vapour trails, marking the sky. 'I think in this and *Totes Meer*', Kenneth Clark told the artist, 'you have discovered a new form of allegorical painting. It is impossible to paint great events without allegory . . . and you have discovered a way of making the symbols out of the events themselves.'

Highlands and Glens

"This spectacular scenery with its breathtaking mountain ranges, beautiful lochs and idyllic silver beaches was ignored at the time landscape painting was establishing its hold in England in the Lakes and the South."

Scotland and England have always had an uneasy relationship. I once made the mistake of saying to an Edinburgh audience that Scotland had agreed to the Act of Union in 1707 – only to be greeted with a howl of disapproval, the Scottish parliament having been, in the eyes of many Scots, coerced into Union. It taught me to tread warily when dealing with Scottish politics. I have since travelled all over the country reporting on nationalism in Scotland and found an ambivalence about Scotland's place in the United Kingdom. It was from the Scots themselves that I first heard about Scottish cringe, the feeling that in some way, which I have never understood, Scotland felt insecure about its identity and its proper place in the modern world.

You only have to travel to Glasgow or Edinburgh and the great Lowland belt between to be puzzled by this. Here, after all, is a place with a clear identity and a thriving energetic culture. It must be galling to the Scots to be defined in the minds of the modern tourist industry as a land of kilts and bagpipes, whisky and

haggis – the clichés of the travel brochures which suggest that, the two great cities aside, Scotland means the Highlands. It is odder still when you think of the contribution that Scotland made during the Scottish Enlightenment with David Hume and Adam Smith revolutionalising eighteenth-century thought.

But leaving politics aside, it is true that the Scotland we know through painting and writing is largely based on the landscape and culture of the Highlands, and their discovery is a relatively recent phenomenon. This spectacular scenery with its breathtaking mountain ranges, beautiful lochs and idyllic silver beaches was ignored at the time landscape painting was establishing its hold in England in the Lakes and the South. Today visitors flock to the Highlands, but two hundred years ago they were still thought to be inaccessible, inhospitable and even downright dangerous. It was not until the end of the eighteenth century and the beginning of the nineteenth that artists and writers, Sir Walter Scott paramount among them, began to transform the image of Scotland by writing sympathetically about Highlands and Lowlands but in a way that would heal the animosity between Scotland and England.

Scott is neglected by modern readers, but in the *Waverley* novels and poems like *The Lady of the Lake* (1810) he created a romantic portrait of 'the land of the mountain and the flood'. I took a boat out to Ellen's Island in the middle of Loch Katrine. It was famous as the place where an English soldier who had swum out to investigate a group of Jacobite women taking refuge there was decapitated. But Scott used it as the romantic setting for his lyric poem in which the Scottish King James V is out hunting when he discovers the exiled Douglas and his beautiful

OPPOSITE
Wild Cotton grows on a peat bog plateau above Glens Afric and Strahfarrar in the Highlands

Jack Butler Yeats (1871–1957), *Morning after Rain* 1923

daughter Ellen living idyllically on an enchanted island. The poem was an instant hit. Tourists flocked to Loch Katrine to see the place for themselves. According to a local resident the roads were filled with horse-drawn carriages, all the inns were crowded to suffocation and every foot of the Loch was 'traversed by travellers carrying copies of the book in their hands ... repeating passages from it with unfeigned rapture.'

Most prominent among the visitors was Queen Victoria who travelled there, book in hand, with Prince Albert. But her predecessor George IV had paid a royal visit to Edinburgh in 1822, a spectacular fifteen days of pageantry choreographed by Walter Scott. The monarch donned the kilt, and was greeted by thousands of Highlanders all in tartan and armed with pistols swords and axes. The streets of Edinburgh were transformed into

a Highland fantasy. Walter Scott had kickstarted the Scottish tourist industry. Queen Victoria, however, set the seal of royal approval on Scotland which has lasted to the present day. She built her castle at Balmoral, had Albert design a Balmoral tartan for wallpaper, chairs and carpets, ate porridge and even, it was said, adopted a Scottish accent on her annual visits. For her the Highlands 'seemed to breathe freedom and peace, and to make one forget the world and its sad turmoils.'

There is another island, the Lake Isle of Innisfree, which inspired the same feelings in the Irish poet W.B. Yeats. I had learnt the poem as a child and the idea of this island with its 'nine bean rows ... and a hive for the honey bee' had always appealed to me. 'I shall have some peace there', Yeats wrote, and his words have calmed many a troubled mind. I went there by boat across Lough

Gill. To tell the truth, it looked a little on the small side even for a dedicated escapist. Barely room to build the hut of clay and wattles. But, like Victoria reciting *The Lady of the Lake* on the shores of Loch Katrine, I found myself repeating Yeats's words as we circled the island.

Yeats's younger brother Jack was a cartoonist and illustrator of children's books but in his middle years concentrated on painting, inspired by his childhood in Sligo. The 'country of open skies, green hills, and stretches of water in lough and sea' made him a painter, he told a friend, and his pictures of Irish life, the travelling fairs and circuses as well as the beaches and mountains, established him as Ireland's first national painter.

Yeats's work is matched by a Northern Irish Protestant, Paul Henry, who had fled the claustrophobia of Belfast to paint in Paris.

Paul Henry (1876–1958), *On Killary Bay, Connemara* c.1930–9

In 1910 he came back to Ireland for a holiday on Achill, a barren windswept island off the western coast, tore up his return ticket and stayed for nine years. He had difficulty painting local people at first – they were superstitious about their images being captured, but he managed to chronicle the tough local life and the dramatic world in which it took place.

I had gone to Innisfree to trace the connections between Scotland and Ireland, both countries with turbulent histories and a fractious relationship with England. The excitement of seeing Innisfree and then travelling out to Achill Island on the west coast matched the thrill of exploring the Scottish Highlands. There have been movements of people between the two countries

Glencar Lake, County Sligo

I wander by the edge –
Of this desolate lake –
Where the wind cries
in the sedge
W. B. YEATS

since the fourth century when the Gaelic 'Scotti' people settled in the Highlands, to the movement of Protestant Scots in the seventeenth century and of Highlanders in the nineteenth during their eviction from their crofts during the Clearances. Both countries have created powerful identities which resonate today and which anyone trying to understand the complex nature of our sometimes disunited Kingdom needs to understand.

Keem Bay, Achill Island, County Mayo

'Land of the Mountain and the Flood'

CHRISTINE RIDING

For many people worldwide, the Highland region *is* Scotland. Nowhere is this better demonstrated than with the iconic status of Edwin Landseer's *Monarch of the Glen* (1851) and Horatio McCulloch's *My Heart's in the Highlands* (1860). As explored elsewhere in this book, it is by no means unusual for a nation to adopt a 'rural face' in reaction to urbanisation and industrialisation. But why, to a large extent, the Scots have located their national identity in the landscape, emblems, costumes and associations of this region – especially one formerly perceived by Lowlanders and non-Scots alike as barren, forbidding and uncivilised – is a result of a more particular history: that of their relationship with England. It was the formation of the United Kingdom of Great Britain by the Act of Union of 1707 that gave this way of picturing the Highland landscape its unique force. The consequent sense of crisis concerning the nation's independence and cultural distinctness resulted in a far greater concern during the eighteenth century to identify and preserve what was unique and separate about Scotland. The outcome was a merger of Highland and Scottish identities during the Romantic period, which reached its apogee in the reign of Queen Victoria (1837–1901). The Highland myth, fostered by British royalty and social elite, found its most potent visual expression in landscapes of historical and literary association or awe-inspiring wilderness. So much so that, by the mid-nineteenth century, these paintings – seemingly devoid of narrative or specific meaning – could be seen to express not only the outward appearance of rural Scotland but also the very spirit of the nation.

THE ACT OF UNION AND HIGHLAND CULTURE

Scotland's increased economic prosperity depended on the Union with England. But there were misgivings both sides of the border. Aggrieved by the loss of the nation's ancient independence, many Scots felt that

David Young Cameron (1865–1945), *Wilds of Assynt c.*1936 (detail)

Horatio McCulloch (1805–1867), *My Heart's in the Highlands* 1860

England's political and material dominance made total assimilation all but inevitable. As the eighteenth century progressed this fear of Anglicisation (primarily in the Lowlands) directed attention towards the Highlands for the means to promote national differences. The term 'Highlands' had been adopted from the fourteenth century as a way of distinguishing the mountainous regions in social and cultural, as well as geographical, terms from the rest of Scotland. The Highlands had a distinctive landscape, the population had social and cultural links to Ireland, spoke Gaelic ('Scotti' was a classical term used to describe Gaelic-speakers from Ireland and Western Scotland), wore plaid and were governed by a feudalistic system, characterised by the social interdependence between the chief and the clan members. Perceived as primitive, dangerous and existing beyond the control of a progressively centralised state, the region was ripe for assimilation into the rest of the country, especially after the crowns of Scotland and England were united under James VI (James I in England).

This process was brought to a head by the successive support given within the Highland community to the Jacobite cause – which sought to re-establish the Catholic Stuart dynasty – from 1688 to its bloody finale at the battle of Culloden in 1746. In order to quash further insurrection and

Landseer's most famous work was originally painted for the refreshment room of the House of Lords, Westminster. It enshrines the type of thrilling wildness and noble beauty that drew people to the Highlands throughout the nineteenth century and beyond.

Edwin Henry Landseer (1802–1873), *Monarch of the Glen* 1851

advance integration, the victorious British government accelerated the dismantling of Highland culture via the Disarming Act of 1746. The Act forbade Highlanders from assembling and carrying or wearing specific Highland weaponry and costume, described as 'plaid, philapeg, trews . . . tartans or parti-coloured plaid'. The ban on costume, repealed after thirty-five years, is perhaps the most symbolic to subsequent generations, given the emotive association of tartan and clanship. But the most important to the development of the cult of 'Highlandism' was the suppression of the ancient relationship between the chief and clansman, giving way to the financial one of landlord and tenant. The social and economic repercussions of this (as well as other 'modernising' methods) included the notorious Highland Clearances from the 1780s and the subsequent movement of people south and overseas. The function and appearance of the landscape was changed forever. The forced emigration of the Highland community, which greatly increased from the 1840s, was visualised during the Victorian period in paintings such as *The Last of the Clan* (1865) by Thomas Faed. The scene shows an elderly clansman, too frail to travel, being left at the quayside as his family and friends prepare to board a ship. According to Dr Samuel Johnson dramatic social and cultural change had already occurred by 1773. During his tour of the Hebrides of that year, he noted:

> There was perhaps never any change of national manners so quick, so great and so general as that which operated in the Highlands by the late conquest and subsequent laws . . . The clans retain little of their original character. Their ferocity of temper is softened, their military ardour is extinguished, their dignity of independence is depressed, their contempt of government is subdued, and their reverence for their chiefs abated.

The 'old order' of the Highlands, once distinct from the rest of Scotland and Britain, had come to an end. Or had it?

Arguably it was its abolition as a specific regional culture, that created the conditions by which Highland culture and by association Highland landscape came to characterise Scotland and Scottishness. Its fate epitomised what many feared: that Scotland itself was dissolving into 'Britain'. As a result, the process of collecting and documenting the largely oral tradition of Highland and Lowland folklore, poetry and ballads, was made

The Last of the Clan by Thomas Faed shows an elderly clansman, too frail to travel, being left at the quayside as his family and friends prepare to board a ship.

Thomas Faed (1826–1900), *The Last of the Clan* 1865

The Glenfinnan Monument at Loch Shiel

increasingly urgent. James Macpherson's *Fragments of Ancient Poetry, Collected in the Highlands of Scotland* (1760) and Walter Scott's *The Minstrelsy of the Scottish Border* (1802–3) are two examples of this impulse. And it gave a specific context and poignancy to the use of Scots dialect in the fictional and poetical work of Scott and Robert Burns. But to make the Highlands 'acceptable', allowing the region to answer the emotional need of a separate national identity without destabilising the Union, a degree of rehabilitation, reworking and mythologising was necessary. As the perceived threat of Jacobitism died away, so its history became the stuff of romantic legend, nationally and internationally; a heroic lost cause (as it turned out) led by 'Bonnie Prince Charlie' in which clan members had played an integral role. As the historian Tom Devine has argued, while clanship was being dismantled in Scotland, its values and structures lived on within the British army. Previously seen as unruly and rebellious, the clansmen as British soldiers were now celebrated for their courage and loyalty, their warlike spirit redirected in defense of Britain and the pursuit of Empire.

Henry Raeburn's portrait of Francis MacNab, a Highland chief and Major in the 1st Battalion (Breadalbane Highlanders), with the brooding drama of the Highland landscape in the background, shows an elderly man full of pride and grim determination.

Henry Raeburn (1756–1823), *Francis MacNab, 'The MacNab'* exhibited 1819

And while the wearing of Highland costume and accoutrements, including bagpipes, had been banned temporarily in Scotland, the Highland regiments were exempt. Thus imbued with sartorial glamour and romantic heroism, these regiments, greatly increased in number from the mid-eighteenth century, were significant in changing attitudes within Britain and overseas towards the Highlands as well as promoting tartan as a national symbol. From the 1760s, there developed a vogue for grand manner portraiture with male sitters in tartan or regimental uniform, a far cry from the scrawny, desperate figure of a plaid-wearing Jacobite in the foreground of Hogarth's celebrated painting *O the Roast Beef of Old England* (1748). Henry Raeburn executed a number of spectacular full-length portraits, with the sitter against a display of Scottish weaponry, as in *Colonel Macdonell of Glengarry* (1812), or exploiting all the brooding drama of the Highland landscape as the background setting. His powerful portrait of Francis MacNab, a Highland chief and Major in the 1st Battalion (Breadalbane Highlanders), shows an elderly man full of pride and grim determination. At the Royal Academy exhibition in 1819, it was described by one critic as a painting 'in which the national character and costume are represented with great truth and vigour'.

THE SCOTTISH ENLIGHTENMENT

Fundamental to this process of revision and rehabilitation was the intellectual flowering known as the Scottish Enlightenment. The Enlightenment, of course, was a European phenomenon and its thinking included the scholarly investigation of 'primitive' civilisations of the past with the aim of finding more virtuous and socially cohesive alternatives to the increasingly urban, industrialised and socially alienated present. In a climate such as this, Highland (and Lowland) folk traditions would be of intellectual interest, at the very least. The fact that there was a 'Scottish' Enlightenment – centred on the capital of Edinburgh – underlines firstly the calibre of the participants, such as the philosopher David Hume and the economist Adam Smith, secondly the Societies, Academies and personal relationships instigated by and between them, and thirdly, that aspects of their activity had a national agenda, including the creation of an Academy of Art. Crucial to the course of Scottish art and to landscape

David Octavius Hill (1802–1870), *A View of Edinburgh from North of the Castle* 1859

painting in particular, the Scottish Enlightenment was marked by the integration of fine artists within this group of intellectuals, putting them on equal terms with internationally renowned historians, antiquarians, poets, philosophers and scientists. From the middle decades of the eighteenth century, Scottish art entered the European mainstream with the careers of Jacob More and Alexander Nasmyth in landscape, Allan Ramsay (son of the celebrated early Enlightenment poet) and Henry Raeburn in portraiture, Gavin Hamilton and John and Alexander Runciman in history painting and James Gibbs and Robert Adam in architecture. All of them, as part of their professional development, travelled on a Grand Tour, studying or practising in Rome. Not surprisingly, their work (with the exception of Raeburn's) reflected the European wide influence of classicism.

In 1766, due to the increased economic prosperity of the city, a competition was held for the design of the so-called New Town in Edinburgh, won by the architect James Craig. The New Town, in contrast to the organic, rambling medieval Old Town, became a visual statement of Enlightenment reason, progress and improvement and the climax of what the art historian Murdo Macdonald has described as 'the great classical architectural project of eighteenth-century Scotland'. The city was physically and intellectually the 'Athens of the North' and increasingly visited by tourists and artists alike, who appreciated its elegant streets and squares and spectacular, panoramic viewpoints. David Octavius Hill,

David Octavius Hill pictured Edinburgh from Castle Rock, contrasting the background of streets and clusters of buildings, bathed in light, with the sombre shadows of the castle in the foreground.

better known today as an early photographer, pictured the city in highly romanticised terms from Castle Rock, contrasting the background of streets and clusters of buildings, bathed in light, with the sombre shadows of the castle in the foreground. Interestingly, Edinburgh emerged from the eighteenth century as a city of contrasts – both old and new, historic and progressive – symbolising in stone the conundrum facing the Scots as they forged a distinct cultural identity. Should the nation look forward or back? In keeping with European trends, landscapes by Scottish artists absorbed the work of seventeenth-century artists, in particular the classicists Claude Lorrain and Nicholas Poussin. Thus parallels can be made between the work of John Knox and Alexander Nasmyth and that of the Welsh artist Richard Wilson (see pp.202, 203), in reconciling British topography with a classical Arcadia. Beyond stylistic considerations, landscape painting also reflected the philosophical enquiry, characteristic of the Enlightenment, into the relationship between society, architecture and landscape. While the castle is the central feature of Nasmyth's composition *Castle Huntly, Perthshire* (*c*.1810), its scale and situation allow it to blend into, rather than dominate, the landscape, creating a scene of aesthetic balance and harmony.

Alexander Nasmyth (1758–1840), *Castle Huntly, Perthshire c.*1810

William McTaggart (1835–1910), *The Emigrants* 1883–9

What makes artistic responses to the Scottish landscape so compelling, however, is the way in which they both engaged with and contributed to international trends and resonated with historical and literary associations and meanings. Jacob More's series of works representing the Falls of Clyde (1771–3), not only imbued the Scottish landscape with the grandeur of Claude or his Italian contemporary Salvator Rosa, but depict a location which was associated with a national hero, William Wallace. While Wallace, as a patriot and freedom fighter, had never disappeared from the national consciousness, such historical figures and events and the locations associated with them rose in value after the Union, as the Scots grappled with its political and cultural implications. In 1784, for example, Robert Burns linked the notion of the landscape of association and his role as a national poet, noting that his native region was

> famous both in ancient and modern times for a gallant and warlike race of inhabitants; a country where civil, and particularly religious liberty have ever found their first support, and their last asylum . . . and the scene of many important events recorded in Scottish history, particularly a great many of the actions of the glorious Wallace, the Saviour of his country.

To Burns and others, the Jacobite cause was not the renegade attempt to replace the Protestant succession with a Catholic, absolute monarchy, but the last in a long history of confrontations in which Scottish patriots fought to retain national independence. Burns's poem *March to Bannockburn* (1793) more popularly known by its opening words 'Scots wha hae', was probably inspired by the 1745 rebellion thus conflating Scottish nationalism with Jacobitism. Given Burns's nationalist stance, it is worth noting that Horatio McCulloch's *The Emigrant's Dream of His Highland Home*, clearly a reference to the ongoing Clearances that began post-Culloden, was renamed in the 1860s after it was engraved as an illustration to Burns's nostalgic song *My Heart's in the Highlands* (1789). The third verse of the song describes both the yearning felt by the emigrant for his native land and its landscape:

> Farewell to the mountains high cover'd with snow;
> Farewell to the straths and green valleys below;
> Farewell to the forrests and wild-hanging woods;
> Farewell to the torrents and loud-pouring floods.

THE SPIRIT OF PLACE

The union of national identity and the landscape was given an ancient 'historical' context with the publication of the epic poems of Ossian, a legendary Gaelic warrior and bard of the third century. Encouraged by the critical reception of *Fragments of Ancient Poetry* in 1760, James Macpherson toured the Highlands, including Skye and the Outer Hebrides, gathering poems and songs from local communities. These were compiled, translated into English and then published as *Fingal* (1762) and *Temora* (1763) each described by Macpherson as 'An Ancient Epic Poem ... composed by Ossian the Son of Fingal'. Elegiac in tone, they chronicle the doomed world of the ancient 'Scottish' warrior-king, Fingal, forming a heady mix of invasion, liberation, heroism, love and loss. The sudden appearance of these poems was greeted with astonishment and delight. Even speculation over the authenticity of Macpherson's translations did nothing to stem the tide of Ossianism which swept Britain, Europe and beyond. Perceived as a voice of original genius, a primal force of Nature and the great poet of loss and

Fingal's Cave, Staffa

isolation, Ossian bridged the Enlightenment and the Romantic movement, as can be seen in numerous artistic responses to the text and the figure of Ossian himself. The poems were translated into eleven languages and inspired writers, poets, artists and composers well into the nineteenth century. But for many Scots, Ossian was also the 'Scottish Homer' – a reference that drew parallels with revered classical civilisations – whose epic poetry fostered the idea of an ancient Gaelic (Celtic) culture in Scotland that predated and contrasted with the dominant Anglo-Saxon literary tradition in Britain.

Significantly, Macpherson was not only a scholar of classical poetry and 'man of the Enlightenment': he was a Highlander by birth and had grown up in the Gaelic-speaking area of Badenoch. More importantly, his uncle, the Clan Chief Ewan Macpherson of Cluny, had joined forces with the Jacobite army in 1745. Thus Macpherson had witnessed the defeat in battle and subsequent disgrace of his clan, the confiscation of their lands and the enforced suppression of Highland culture. Macpherson promoted the Highlanders through Ossian as the direct descendants of the ancient Gaels, who, as legend had it, were the only inhabitants of Britain to resist

Locations made famous by Ossian, in particular Fingal's Cave, were not only appreciated for their primal, untamed beauty but also stood testament to Scotland's ancient cultural heritage, its patriotism and independence.

Roman Imperial rule. As such, their isolation (as he described it) 'among the mountains and inaccessible parts of a country' was considered a virtue in maintaining their position as 'pure', authentic Scots. And their way of life and folklore constituted an unbroken link between the remote past and the near present. Locations made famous by Ossian, in particular Fingal's Cave, were not only appreciated for their primal, untamed beauty but, by extension, stood testament to Scotland's ancient cultural heritage, its patriotism and independence.

Off the Western Hebrides, on the remote uninhabited island of Staffa, Fingal's Cave was 'rediscovered' by the Enlightenment botanist and traveller Sir Joseph Banks in 1772. By this point (according to Banks) the site had already become associated with Finn or Fingal of legend and Macpherson's Ossian. This unique sea-cave is formed completely in hexagonally-jointed basalt with a 227-foot cavern. In his travel journal *A Cruise around Scotland in 1814*, Walter Scott described his experience on entering the cave:

> The stupendous columnar side walls – the depth and strength of the ocean with which the cavern is filled – the variety of tints formed by stalactites dropping and petrifying between the pillars . . . the dreadful noise of those august billows so well corresponding with the grandeur of the scene – are all circumstances elsewhere unparalleled.

This dramatic 'spirit of place' is conveyed in the stirring arrangement of Felix Mendelssohn's celebrated 'Hebrides Overture: Fingal's Cave' composed after a visit to Staffa in 1829 and first performed in London in 1832. In the same year, J.M.W. Turner exhibited an atmospheric inter-pretation of the island viewed from the sea, showing a paddle steamer, such as he and other tourists had travelled on, approaching the mouth of the cave. Thus the Ossianic landscape offered a specific way of viewing or imagining the landscape. In the case of Glencoe this mythic association was combined with historical fact. In his influential *Observations on Several Parts of Great Britain, particularly the Highlands of Scotland*, published in 1776, William Gilpin noted that the 'valley of Glencoe [was] famous . . . for being the birth-place of Ossian. In its wild scenes that bard is said to have caught his first poetic raptures. Near lies the country of Morven; which Fingal hath turned into classic ground by his huntings, and his wars.' He also noted that the area was notorious for the massacre in 1692 of members of the McDonald clan by those of the Campbell clan. The

OVERLEAF
The peaks of the Blackmount Estate from Lochain nah Achlaise Rannoch Moor

My heart's in the Highlands, my heart is not here,
My heart's in the Highlands a-chasing the deer –
A-chasing the wild deer, and following the roe;
My heart's in the Highlands, wherever I go.
ROBERT BURNS (1759–96)

Thomas Miles Richardson (1813–1890), *Glencoe* 1853

McDonald chief had initially refused and then belatedly submitted to the
Act of Succession. The McDonalds' resistance to tyranny – as they saw it –
and the subsequent action of the Campbells under orders from the King
William III, constituted an emotive episode in the history of the Jacobite
cause and united for eternity the Highland scenery, to use Gilpin's words,
'abounding with beauties of the most romantic kind' with an event 'of
horrid cruelty and treachery'. Given these associations, it is impossible to
view any representation of Glencoe, such as Thomas Miles Richardson's
watercolour, as simply an atmospheric landscape. And the spirit of the
past was not only evoked by the printed word, oral tradition or historic
man-made structures, in particular castles, but in the nineteenth century
was indelibly marked on the landscape by the building of battlefield cairns
and monuments, a process that has continued to the present day. In 1815,
for example, the Glenfinnan Monument at Loch Shiel (see p.95), where the
1745 rebellion began, was erected 'in tribute to the clansmen who fought
and died in the cause of Prince Charles Edward Stuart'. And in 1869, the
Wallace Monument, replete with a Hall of Heroes, was built at Abbey
Cairn near Stirling, the site of Wallace's victory against English forces
in 1297. Both monuments command spectacular views of the Highlands.

O Caledonia! stern and wild,
Meet nurse for a poetic child!
Land of brown heath and
shaggy wood, Land of the
mountain and the flood,
Land of my sires! what mortal
hand Can e'er untie the filial
band, That knits me to thy
rugged strand!

WALTER SCOTT,
The Lay of the Last Minstrel

SIR WALTER SCOTT

The landscape of association was given its most influential expression through Walter Scott. Scott's work, characterised by strongly visual narrative and romantic realism, caused an international clamour, more so than any other writer of the period. But what did he do for Scotland? The fact that the phrase 'Scott country' is current today is perhaps an indication. And Abbotsford, Scott's appropriately styled 'Scottish baronial' mansion on the river Tweed, remains a popular tourist destination. Over the course of his career, Scott wrote seven novels with Scottish settings, three with a Jacobite theme – *Waverley* (1814), *Rob Roy* (1818) and *Redgauntlet* (1824) – as well as verse narratives such as the *Lady of the Lake* (1810). Sometimes described as a 'Union-nationalist', Scott's view on post-Union Scotland was that despite the gains, much had been lost. He attempted to reconcile this somewhat paradoxical point of view by acknowledging Anglo-Scottish conflict and expressing a sense of regret, but without an aggressive nationalist agenda. And thus, instead of Burns's more defiant promotion of Scottish distinctness he offered instead a safe, sentimental nationalism that was adopted throughout the nineteenth century and arguably beyond.

While Scotland had entered the British and European consciousness in the eighteenth century through Ossian or writers like Gilpin, there was something original and immediate about Scott's approach. In his published journal, Henry Cockburn recollected the impact that Scott's first novel, *Waverley*, had had on its public: 'The unexpected newness of the thing, the profusion of original characters, the Scotch language, Scotch scenery, Scotch men and women, the simplicity of the writing, the graphic force of the descriptions, all struck us with an electric shock of delight.' This impact was not isolated to Scotland, or Britain, but was international. Albeit increasingly a destination for British tourists, especially when the French Revolution and Napoleonic Wars made the Continent largely inaccessible, Scott, more than any other person, put Scotland on the map. The historian Alastair Durie has stated that 1810, the year Scott's *Lady of the Lake* was published, 'has a real claim to be one of the decisive dates in the development of Scottish tourism.' 20,000 copies were sold in the first year, resulting in a dramatic rise in visitors to locations such as Loch Katrine, which transformed the Trossachs into a premier-league tourist destination. John Knox's painting of Loch Katrine gives an idea of tourism in the early

John Knox (1778–1845), *Landscape with Tourists at Loch Katrine* c.1820s

nineteenth century, with visitors standing at the lakeside, their Highland experience no doubt augmented by the presence of a tartan-clad piper. The same was true of Scottish locations featured in other published works such as *Heart of Midlothian*, *Rob Roy* and so on. A crucial part of the 'Walter Scott phenomenon' and the progress of Highlandism was not only the wealth of artistic responses, often exhibited in London, Edinburgh, Paris and elsewhere, or published as illustrations, but the tremendous vogue for dramatising Scott's verse narratives and novels. Thus through Scott, the noble savagery of the Highlands entered the urban theatres and opera houses of Europe. The *Lady of the Lake*, for example, was first staged by Thomas J. Dibdin at the Surrey theatre, London, in the same year of publication, after which more than 200 distinct productions of plays, operas (including Giacomo Rossini's *La Donna del Lago*, first performed in 1819) and dramatic derivatives can be listed. Significantly the scenery and thus the landscape was often more heavily promoted in the playbills than, for example, the music.

ROYALTY AND BALMORALISATION

Exactly how far Highlandism had come in the seventy or so years after the 1745 rebellion is demonstrated by King George IV's visit to Edinburgh in 1822. This was the first visit by a reigning monarch since the Hanoverian dynasty came to the British throne in 1714. Significantly, it was stage managed by Walter Scott. *All* participants wore 'clan' tartans, most of which appear to have been devised for the occasion. And at the height of this extraordinary pageant – clearly an imaginative concoction of fact and fiction – the King gave a toast to 'the chieftains and clans of Scotland'. However the 'Highland takeover' (to use the historian Hugh Trevor-Roper's phrase) was by no means endorsed by all Scots. As one contemporary commentator stated, 'a great mistake was made by the stage managers – one that offended all the southern Scots; the King wore at the levee the Highland dress. I dare say he thought that country all Highland, expected no fertile plains, and did not know the difference between the Saxon and the Celt.' In London, both the King and his friend Sir William Curtis, formerly the Mayor of London, took a lampooning via caricatures, such as George Cruikshank's *Geordie and Willie*. Corpulent and ludicrous, 'Willie'

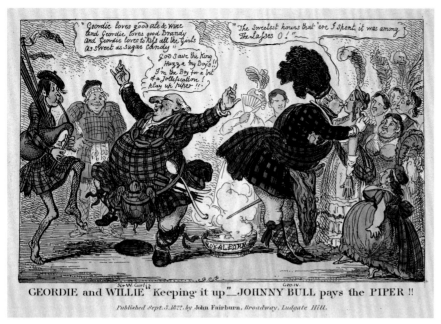

George Cruikshank (1792–1878), *Geordie and Willie "keeping it up" – Johnny Bull Pays the Piper* 1822

attempts a Highland jig and 'Geordie' kisses a startled lady, the speech bubble above his head misquoting Burns's love song, *Green Grow the Rashes O* (1783). But despite such protests and ridicule, now that the Highland myth as Scottish national identity had been given the Royal seal of approval, the 'takeover' seemed unstoppable, at least within the British social elite. In his book *Highland Games: The Making of the Myth*, Grant Jarvie has noted that the national transformation represented by George IV's visit contributed to the next phase of Highlandism – the emergence of the sporting landlord, the popularisation of the Highland Gathering and the process of 'Balmoralisation'. At the centre of it all was Queen Victoria, who from the 1840s onwards displayed a deep affinity with the Highlands, initially as a tourist and then as a landowner. In 1844, she wrote in her journal:

> The English coast appeared terribly flat. Lord Aberdeen was quite touched when I told him I was so attached to the dear dear Highlands and missed the fine hills so much. There is a great peculiarity about the Highlands and the Highlanders; and they are such a chivalrous, fine, active people. Our stay amongst them was delightful. Independently of the beautiful scenery, there was a quiet, a retirement, a wilderness, a liberty and solitude that has a charm for us.

In 1848, the year she purchased the Balmoral estate, the Queen, her consort Prince Albert and members of the Court attended the Highland Gathering of the Braemar Society, an event that was to be hosted at Balmoral itself in subsequent years. The Queen even acted as Highland chieftain to the Gathering, a tradition involving the reigning monarch to

Gourlay Steell (1819–1894), *A Highland Parting* 1885

Gourlay Steell's painting is emblematic of the formulaic representation of the Highlands produced by both Scottish and English artists in the late nineteenth century. It was such clichés as the windswept wilderness, rustics, tartan and shaggy livestock that spurred Scottish artists to find alternative landscapes and subjects.

Michael Andrews (1928–1995), *Alistair's Day: 2nd Stalk* 1980

this day. The resurgence of the Highland Gatherings (or Games) in general
was given a tremendous boost by the participation of the royal family. But
the bonding of Balmoral and Braemar not only characterised Scotland's
relationship with the monarch as a derivation of ancient clanship, but
also promoted the idea of Scotland as a sporting playground. The most
resonant field sport, in terms of Highlandism, Scottish national identity
and associated imagery, was deer hunting. Its enthusiastic endorsement by
Queen Victoria and Prince Albert is underlined by Edwin Landseer's large-
scale painting, *Royal Sports on Hill and Loch*, which was a royal commission.
Stalking and shooting deer in the Highlands had occurred before the
Victorian period. But what marked the nineteenth century from the past
was the creation of deer forests as private sporting estates. As with salmon
fishing and grouse shooting, these were largely developed by the Lowland
and English social elites (both the traditional aristocracy and the *nouveau
riches*). By 1912, deer forests covered one fifth of the Scottish land area.

As a primordial contest between man and Nature, the subject of hunting
and images of wild life and game had been important themes in British
and European art since at least the eighteenth century. Before Landseer,
the best-known practitioner is the eighteenth-century artist George

Stubbs (pp.126, 151). More recently, Michael Andrews has produced a series of paintings on the subject of deer stalking in Scotland, including *Alistair's Day: 2nd Stalk* (1980). His paintings are less a celebration of an elite sport and more a commentary on a time-honoured human activity in association with a specific location. 'Actually what I'm painting', the artist explained, 'is historical landscape, that's to say landscape relating to the chain of events. It's time and landscape that interests me.' Given the social and economic backdrop to the creation of deer parks from the Victorian period, in particular the Clearances and the hardships endured by crofters, it still seems ironic that the deer, or more specifically, the stag in the Highland landscape has come to rival the tartan-clad Highlander as a symbol of the Scottish nation. But the social and cultural forces that transformed the Highlander and the stag were arguably the same. In the paintings of Landseer, the stag becomes heroic: as much a symbol of Nature's primal power as the Highland landscape itself. And the stag, like the Highlander, is imbued with nostalgia and fatalism. The haunting image of deer in an isolated landscape stood testimony to the actual process of de-population and promoted to urban audiences, especially in London, the romantic notion of the Highlands as a windswept wilderness. This emphasis on isolation can be seen in the landscapes *Chill October* (1870) and *Glen Birnam* (1891) by the English artist John Everett Millais, who was himself an avid hunter and fisherman in Scotland. *Chill October* is particularly contrived, as the location was viewable from the train between Perth and Dundee.

ART AND HIGHLANDISM

Was the preeminence of romantic Highlandism ever challenged? Certainly by Scottish artists. In the late nineteenth century, attempts were made to challenge what was by the 1880s a formulaic representation of the Highlands produced by the Art establishment, by innovations in technique, colour palate and composition. Scottish artists like George Reid took contemporary French and Dutch landscape paintings as their cue and focused on rural scenes from Lowland Scotland. Similar influences and ambitions informed the so-called Glasgow Boys, such as John Lavery, James Guthrie and Edward Arthur Walton, who purposely focused on non-Highland subject matter. Walton's *Berwickshire Field-Workers* (1884) is

in every sense a rebuttal to Gourlay Steell's *A Highland Parting* (1885)
in which, to quote the art historian John Morrison, the artist has put
'as many clichés about Scots and Highland culture as he could unearth.'
William McTaggart produced a group of seascapes known as the 'Emigrant
ship' paintings. With their free brushwork and concentration on texture
and light, these works stand in complete contrast to McCulloch's *My Heart's
in the Highlands,* albeit inspired by the same subject, and represent a
highly original interpretation of the Highland Clearances as an historical
phenomenon. And the Highland landscape is given a new vigour and
boldness in the hands of the Scottish Colourist, Samuel John Peploe, in
works such as *Green Sea, Iona* (1925) and David Young Cameron, in the
Wilds of Assynt (c.1936). But, unlike the work of McCulloch, neither of
these paintings are nostalgic.

Perhaps the emphasis on appealing to collective nostalgia is why
romantic Highlandism has prevailed, despite the international outlook
and dynamism of much of twentieth- and twenty-first-century Scottish
art. But the artistic clichés of Highlandism have been challenged and
parodied by British contemporary artists. Peter Blake's *After the Monarch of*

David Young Cameron (1865–1945), *Wilds of Assynt c.*1936

Edward Arthur Walton (1860–1922), *Berwickshire Field-Workers* 1884

the Glen by Edwin Landseer (1966) transforms the original painting into a piece of Pop art, thus visualising its transcendence as a national icon, which, as Michael Compton has noted, 'like pop stars, has an existence in the media separate from itself.' In the 1960s, a whole generation of artists emerged who sought to find new ways of engaging with the subject of landscape. For example, the art form for Hamish Fulton is the walk made within the landscape. The 'artwork' that is produced subsequently – whether photographic or printed – has a secondary status, on the basis that 'an object cannot compete with an experience'. From 1971, he has made numerous walks through the Scottish Cairngorms. *All* Fulton's work emphasises the unique and finite nature of his experience. But the works which use text only completely reject the visual conventions associated with the Highlands.

SEVEN DAYS WALKING AND SEVEN NIGHTS CAMPING IN A WOOD SCOTLAND MARCH 1985

SOUND OF THE STREAM ■ NO BIRDS SINGING ■ DAWN ■ BIRDS SINGING ■ NO BIRDS SINGING ■ SOUND OF THE STREAM ■ FALLEN TREES ACROSS THE STREAM ■ WHITE ROCKS ■ GREY DRY RIVERBED ROCKS ■ PEBBLES ■ SAND ■ PINE NEEDLES ■ PINE CONES ■ STONES ■ SOUND OF THE STREAM ■ DEAD TREES ■ FALLEN TREES ■ FALLEN BRANCHES ON A DEER PATH ■ NO BIRD SONG ■ WIND THROUGH THE PINE TREES ■ ROUNDED MOUNTAINS ■ WIND BLOWN CLOUDS ■ RAIN SHOWER ■ SNOWFALL ■ PINE NEEDLES ■ SAND ■ WET GROUND ■ MELTED SNOW ■ BROWN BARK ■ GREY BARK ■ FALLEN BARK ON A DEER PATH ■ DEER TRACKS ON THE SAND ■ BIRD SONG HEARD IN THE SOUND OF THE STREAM ■ SPLASHED ROCKS ■ DRY GREY RIVERBED ROCKS ■ ROTTING TREES ■ MOSS COVERED BOULDERS ■ ANTHILLS ■ SMALL LANDSLIDE ■ WHITE ROCKS ■ WET ROCKS ■ RUSHING STREAM AT NIGHT ■ NO BIRD SONG AT NIGHT ■ BIRD SONG AT DAWN ■ NO BIRD SONG ■ GREY CLOUD ■ MOVING MIST OVER THE HILLS ■ POOLS OF WATER ON FLAT ROCK ■ COLD WIND ■ SPLASHED ROCK ■ SAND ■ PINE CONES ■ DEAD BRACKEN ■ OLD RIVERBED ■ NEW ANT HILL ■ ANCIENT ROUNDED MOUNTAINS ■ WHITE HARE ■ SCATTERED WHITE ROCKS ON THE HILLSIDE ■ PTARMIGAN ■ DRY GREY RIVERBED ROCK ■ SPLASHED ROCK ■ WET GROUND ■ BROWN BARK ■ WET TREE ■ BROWN PINE NEEDLES ■ DEER PATH ■ MORNING LIGHT ■ NIGHT SNOWFALL ■ SNOW COVERED SAND ■ SNOW COVERED ROCKS ■ SOUND OF THE STREAM ■ TWIGS IN THE SNOW ■ GREEN PINE NEEDLES ■ BROWN BRACKEN ■ SNOW ON FALLEN TREES ACROSS THE STREAM ■ REEDS ■ SNOW FILLED DEER PATH ■ DEER TRACKS IN THE SNOW ON THE PATH ■ FRESH DEER TRAIL THROUGH THE HEATHER BRUSHING OFF THE SNOW ■ STONES NOT COVERED BY SNOW BELOW A TREE ■ PINE CONES ■ A ROBIN STANDS ON AN ANTHILL ■ A CROW CALLING ■ ROBIN SINGING ■ GREY SKY ■ A FEW SNOWFLAKES FALLING ■ GRASS AND GREEN LEAVES BENEATH OLD TREES ■ GREY TREE TRUNKS BROWN BRANCHES GREEN NEEDLES ■ A PIGEON FLYING BETWEEN THE DEAD TREES ■ GREY SKY ■ BLUE SKY ■ WHITE CLOUDS ■ UPROOTED TREE ■ SNOW ON GREY DEAD BRANCHES ■ GREEN LEAVES ON OLD ANTHILLS ■ PINE NEEDLES ■ MELTING SNOW IN THE MIDDLE OF THE DAY ■ A FEW FLAKES OF FALLING SNOW ■ SUN THROUGH CLOUDS ■ UPROOTED TREE ■ A DEER STANDING STILL LOOKING MOVING DISAPPEARING ■ BIRD SONG ■ MELTING SNOW ■ CRACKED DEAD TREE TRUNKS ■ FALLING SNOW FROM BRANCHES CATCHING THE SUNLIGHT ■ PINE CONES ■ TWIGS ■ PINE NEEDLES ■ SOUND OF THE STREAM ■ MOSS ■ LICHEN ■ MELTING SNOW ■ SNOW ON HEATHER ■ BRANCHES ■ TWIGS ■ MOVING GREY CLOUDS ■ MUDDY SQUIRREL TRACKS IN THE SNOW ■ GREY ROCKS AND GREEN LICHEN ■ BROWN AND GREEN HEATHER ■ DEER DROPPINGS BENEATH THE TREES ■ LIGHT GREEN MOSS ■ BIRD SONG ■ SOUND OF THE STREAM ■ HUNDREDS OF ANTS AMONG THE PINE NEEDLES ■ DEER TRACKS IN THE SNOW ■ DEER DROPPINGS BY AN ANTHILL ■ OLD BRACKEN STALKS ■ MOLEHILL ■ SOUND OF THE STREAM ■ GREY BROWN AND PINK ROCKS ■ ISLANDS OF ROCK IN THE STREAM ■ HALF FALLEN TREES ■ STANDING DEAD TREES ■ REEDS ■ PINE BRANCHES IN THE STREAM ■ BROKEN PINE BRANCHES ■ SNOW CAPPED ROCKS IN THE STREAM ■ SNOW FILLED DEER PATHS WITHOUT DEER TRACKS ■ FEEDING DEER ■ DISAPPEARING DEER ■ DEER TRACKS ON FLAT SNOW COVERED GROUND ■ DEAD GRASS ■ A FEW SNOW FLAKES FALLING ■ OLD TREES ■ DROPS OF WATER FALLING FROM BRANCHES INTO THE SNOW ■ GREEN LEAVES ■ DEAD GRASS ■ WIND THROUGH THE PINE TREES ■ NO SOUND OF THE STREAM ■ DISTANT BIRD SONG ■ ANTHILLS FACING SOUTH ■ SOUND OF THE STREAM ■ SMALL HERDS OF DEER STANDING MOVING DISAPPEARING ■ SUNLIGHT ON THE STREAM ■ WET GROUND ■ AFTERNOON SUNLIGHT ON GREEN PINE NEEDLES AND SNOW ■ LIFE FORCE OF THE STREAM ■ MORE AND MORE WATER PASSING THE ROCKS BY THE STREAM BANK ■ WATER FAST SUN SLOWLY ■ SHADOWS IN THE WATER ■ SOUND OF THE STREAM ■ A CLEAR REPEATED BIRD SONG ■ COLD AIR ■ SMALL BIRD ■ SNOW ON A HILL NOT FACING THE SUN ■ PALE BLUE AND PINK EVENING SKY ■ NO STARS ■ SOUND OF THE STREAM ■ TALL GREEN JUNIPER BUSHES AMONG THE BROWN HEATHER AND GREEN COVERED ANTHILLS ■ LINE OF SNOW ON A FALLEN TREE TRUNK ■ LIGHT THROUGH THE TREES FROM THE WEST ■ PINE CONES ■ TWIGS AND BRANCHES BENEATH AN OLD TREE ■ DEER PATH ■ NO BIRD SONG ■ DUSK ■ SOUND OF THE STREAM ■ DEER TRACKS ON FLAT SNOW COVERED GROUND ■ AN AREA OF SNOW BENEATH PINE TREES ■ GREEN NEEDLES ■ FLECKS OF SNOW AGAINST A PALE BLUE GREY EVENING SKY ■ A BRANCH OVER THE STREAM ■ A BRANCH IN THE STREAM ■ A TALL PINE TREE ■ DRY TOPPED ROCKS IN THE STREAM ■ FOX TRACKS IN THE SNOW THROUGH THE DEAD BRACKEN ■ DARKNESS ■ SOUND OF THE STREAM ■ BRIGHT MORNING SUNLIGHT ON THE FACES OF THE ROCKS IN THE STREAM ■ FLICKERING WATER REFLECTING ON THE SIDES OF THE ROCKS ■ THE REPEATED SONG OF A BIRD ■ A SHOWER OF SUNLIT SNOW FALLING FROM A BRANCH ■ ROCKS IN SHADOW ■ REPEATED BIRD SONG ■ SMALL STREAM ■ WET GROUND ■ DEER ■ DEER RUBBING TREE ■ FRESH DEER TRACKS THROUGH THE BOG ■ OLD TREE ■ SMELL OF DEER ■ CAPERCAILLIE FLYING LOW THROUGH THE TREES ■ WIND BROKEN BRANCH ■ DEER RUBBING BRANCH ■ HAIL ■ CAPERCAILLIE FLYING LOW THROUGH THE TREES ■ NO SOUNDS OF THE BIG STREAM ■ HAIL ■ LIGHT SNOW FALL ■ SOUND OF THE SMALL STREAM ■ WIND BLOWING THROUGH THE PINE TREES ■ COLD EVENING ■ STARS ■ WARMER NIGHT ■ HEAVY SNOWFALL IN THE DARK ■ GREY LIGHT ■ SNOWFLAKES FALLING ■ SNOW ROUNDED HEATHER AND ROCKS ■ ROUNDED SNOW ON PINE BRANCHES ■ SNOW COVERED ANTHILLS ■ SUDDEN LOW FLYING CAPERCAILLIE THROUGH THE TREES ■ SNOW SPRAYED TREE TRUNKS ■ WHITE LINES OF SNOW ON FALLEN TREES ■ A HERD OF DEER SITTING STANDING MOVING SLOWLY RUNNING DISAPPEARING INTO THE SNOW COVERED PINE TREES ■ RUNNING UPHILL ■ DOWNHILL ■ FRESH TRACKS ■ BRANCHES BENT LOW WITH THE WEIGHT OF SNOW ■ IN THE DISTANCE TWO DARK DEER STILL ■ RUNNING ■ FRESH DEER TRACKS ■ DEER LYING PLACES ■ DEER TRACKS ■ SUDDEN DISTURBED CAPERCAILLIE FLAPPING WINGS THROUGH TREES ■ DARK GROUND OF UPROOTED TREES IN THE SNOW ■ FIVE OR SIX DEER RUNNING IN A LINE UPHILL ■ ROUNDED ANTHILLS ■ OLD DEAD PINE TREE ALONE ■ WIND BLOWN SNOWFLAKES SIDEWAYS ■ CROW FLYING IN THE WIND ■ CROW SITTING ON THE TOP OF A TALL PINE TREE CALLING IN THE WIND AND SNOW ■ ROUNDED ANTHILLS ■ ARCHING REEDS ON FLAT GROUND ■ SOUND OF THE STREAM ■ GREY DEAD FALLEN TREES ■ SNOW FILLING DEER TRACKS ■ ROUNDED SNOW ON THE BUSHES ■ LIGHT GREY SKY ■ SNOWING ■ BLUE SKY WHITE SKY GREY SKY ■ SUNSHINE ■ A ROBIN SINGS FROM THE VERY TOP OF A TALL PINE TREE ■ GREY SKY ■ LIGHT SNOWFALL ■ TWO DEER RUN BETWEEN THE SNOW ROUNDED ANTHILLS AND STOP RUN UPHILL INTO THE TREES STOP RUN DISAPPEAR ■ FRESH DEER TRACKS ■ ROUNDED SNOW AT THE VERY EDGE OF THE STREAM ■ FALLEN DEAD TREES ACROSS THE STREAM ■ SNAKING COURSE OF THE STREAM ■ SNOW COVERED ANTHILLS AND BUSHES ■ SNOW COVERED SAND ■ DRY GREY RIVERBED ROCKS ■ ARCHING REEDS ON FLAT GROUND ■ SNOW COVERED TWISTING PINE TREE ON THE SLOPE ■ SNOW SMOOTHED DEER PATH ■ SUDDEN DISTURBED CAPERCAILLIE FLYING LOW THROUGH THE TREES ■ SNOW SMOOTHED DEER PATH CROSSED BY DEER TRACKS FILLING WITH SNOW ■ BRANCHES BENDING WITH THE WEIGHT OF SNOW ■ SOUND OF THE SMALL STREAM ■ SUNSHINE ■ PATCHES OF SUNLIT SNOW ■ ROUNDED ANTHILLS ■ DARK TREE TRUNKS ■ GREY SKY ■ NO SNOW FALLING ■ SOUND OF THE SMALL STREAM ■ PALE GREY PALE BLUE YELLOW SKY IN THE LATE AFTERNOON ■ SMALL HERD OF DEER ONE RUBBING A BRANCH STOP LOOK TURN AND RUN ■ MANY DARK LEGS PASSING TREE TRUNKS ■ UNSEEN DEER BARKING ■ EVENING PALE BLUE SKY BEHIND THE TREES ■ STRAIGHT TREES ■ TWISTED TREES ■ BRANCHES WEIGHED DOWN WITH SNOW ■ GREY TREE TRUNKS LIGHT BROWN BRANCHES GREEN NEEDLES ■ LIGHT FALL OF HAIL ■ COLD ■ STILL ■ SOUND OF THE STREAM ■ PALE BRIGHT SUNLIGHT ■ SETTING SUN BETWEEN THE TREES ■ A FEW SNOWFLAKES FALLING ■ NO SNOWFLAKES FALLING ■ SNOWING ■ GREY SKY ■ NO SNOW FALLING ■ SOUND OF THE SMALL STREAM RUNNING OVER ROCKS INTO POOLS AND ON DOWNHILL TO A BIGGER STREAM ■ DARKNESS ■ NIGHT ■ LIGHT SNOW SHOWERS ■ MORNING BRIGHT SUN THROUGH THE TREES ■ BLUE SKY ■ SUN MELTING SNOW IN THE TREES ■ SNOW FALLS FROM THE BRANCHES ■ WARMTH FROM THE SUN ■ A BRIGHT BLUE CLOUDLESS SKY ■ FALLING SNOW FROM THE BRANCHES ■ HOLES IN THE SNOW ON THE GROUND ■ AT THE VERY TOP OF A LIVING TREE A SMALL GREY BREASTED BIRD SINGING A TWO NOTE SONG ■ FOUR SINGLE BARKS FROM AN UNSEEN DEER UP A SLOPE IN THE TREES ■ PALE GREY CLOUDS MOVING OVER THE HILLTOPS

Hamish Fulton (born 1946), *Seven Days Walking and Seven Nights Camping in a Wood, Scotland, March 1985*

Hamish Fulton has made numerous walks in this Highland region. 'I just became addicted to the Cairngorms,' he has said, 'I am attracted by the arctic quality of the tops and the wild character of the remnant forests.' He has also noted over the years the human impact on the environment, describing the Cairgorms as 'a great national treasure in a state of crisis.'

Clouds covering
a Cairngorm plateau

In a more general sense, however, the example of Scott, McCulloch, Landseer and others, in terms of tourism, popular entertainment and the export of a particular vision of Scotland, has exerted a tenacious grip on the national and international consciousness during the twentieth century. This has been sustained through Scotland's National Tourism Board and the National Trust for Scotland, where Highlandism remains a dominant theme in promotional material. This is equally true of the mass visual media of television and cinema (via literary, theatrical or historical adaptations), examples being the pure fantasy world of *Brigadoon*, the Broadway musical adapted as a Hollywood film in 1954, to the more recent release of *Highlander* (1986), *Rob Roy* (1995) and most importantly, in terms of latter day Scottish nationalism, *Braveheart* (1995). And in Britain, what greater tribute to the staying power of Highlandism could there be than the BBC's 'whisky and whimsy' television drama, *Monarch of the Glen*?

The Heart of England

"Towards the end of the eighteenth century the beautiful valleys of Coalbrookdale resounded twenty-four hours a day to the crashing noise of the iron casters at work. Flames and smoke lit up the night sky."

Of all the parts of Britain which make up our Picture, the Heart of England is the most idiosyncratic because it combines some places of breath-taking beauty with the ugliest and most depressing remains of our industrial past. That past is in decline now. The slag heaps are being turned back into green fields and parks, but the traces of the heyday of industry will never be removed.

In the great cities like Manchester, a new and vibrant urban life is replacing the dank streets and gloomy mills which until recently were its hallmark. But in the Black Country it is a struggle to achieve regeneration. Yet when industry was first established it was admired. Few realised the miserable conditions which would come to epitomise life here.

When the Berlin Wall fell and travel was possible once more between the Communist East and the Capitalist West, workers on the land in northern Romania left in droves to work in the factories of Munich. Saxon villages which for centuries had provided a bucolic life for their farmers were deserted. The summer harvest, cut by scythe, the fortified churches with their cured hams hanging in the belfry to provide iron rations in the event of invasion, the geese pecking at the grass on the wide verges were abandoned. When I travelled through this part of Transylvania I wondered whether the swapping of this quiet life for the noisy grind of German cities was a sensible trade-off. But it is a question as easily answered in Romania, or in remote Indian villages for that matter, as it must have been at the start of the Industrial Revolution in England. Given a choice, most people would rather work for cash than for barter, would rather be able to afford luxuries like a car and a television than live at subsistence level.

When Richard Arkwright built his great spinning mills, women and children came to work for him on the long rows of machinery while the men stayed at home to weave. It was an improvement on life in the cottage and a revolution whose logic was irresistible. It is calculated that one person working on one of Arkwright's spinning frames could produce in a day nine hundred times

OPPOSITE Ironbridge Gorge and Buildwas Power Station, Shropshire

Bernd (born 1931) and Hilla Becher (born 1934), *Pitheads* 1974

Edward Wadsworth (1889–1949), *Black Country* 1919

the output of a worker operating a spinning wheel at home. No wonder visitors came from all over Britain to see what Arkwright had achieved – so many that he had to build a hotel to accommodate them.

Arkwright used water power for his factories – what we would now call an environmentally friendly energy source. But the great leap forward came with the use of steam power which drove pumps that freed men to dig deeper into the ground for iron, coal and tin. Towards the end of the eighteenth century the beautiful valleys of Coalbrookdale resounded twenty-four hours a day to the crashing noise of the iron casters at work. Flames and smoke lit up the night sky. It was exciting, romantic and even patriotic to find pleasure in these scenes. Painters like Joseph Wright of Derby and Philip de Louterbourg ('Old Leatherbags', as he was affectionately known) painted powerful images of the new technology which at the start seemed to merge sympathetically into the dramatic crags and rocky outcrops that surrounded it. Innocent days.

But it was not long before others began to count the cost in human terms of this ingenuity. In 1838 Charles Dickens came to the West Midlands and saw just 'rows of chimneys pouring out their smoke'.

He foresaw a time when the people whose lives were being destroyed by the conditions they lived in would rise up and exact a terrible revenge. Towards the end of the century William Morris led a movement to restore the old balance between man and his work. 'Forget six counties overhung with smoke/ Forget the snorting steam and piston stroke/ Forget the spreading of the hideous town/ Think rather of the pack-horse on the down', he wrote. From his Tudor manor house at Kelmscott in the Cotswolds such a vision might have seemed achievable. He even wrote a novel, *News from Nowhere*, in which by the year 2102 England, after a revolution, would have seen central government abolished, half of London returned to grass, and Manchester obliterated altogether.

The Industrial Revolution came and went. We are still picking up the pieces. But the Heart of England which boasts, alongside the industrial wasteland of the Black Country, the glorious countryside stretching from Derbyshire to Shropshire or the Malvern Hills is a reminder of how easily our places can be destroyed. It is a moral for our own careless times.

Industrial chimney,
Snailbeach, Shropshire

OVERLEAF The Malvern Hills

We naturally identify our land-scapes most easily with painting. More elusive is the connection between our countryside and music. And yet there are British composers whose sounds have been, by their own admission, inspired by the places where they lived. The Malvern Hills was home to Edward Elgar who walked and bicycled through the Worcestershire lanes and always claimed it was on these expeditions that his music came to him. 'I am still at heart the dreamy child who used to be found in the reeds by Severn side with a sheet of paper, trying to fix the sounds and longing for something very great', he wrote to a friend in middle age. His music is very English, not because like some identifiably national composers it uses English folk song for its inspira-tion. Elgar was scornful of the notion. As he once said : 'I am folk music'.

Listening to Benjamin Britten it is easy to conjure up images of the Suffolk coast. Or, to take a quite different example, it would be hard to hear Sibelius's *Finlandia* without being transported to the gloomy birch and fir forests of Finland. Listening to Elgar's *Cello Concerto* it is the windswept Malverns with their dramatic views across dark hills of Wales on one side and over the lush Vale of Evesham to the other that fills the imagination. Does music really sound like the places it comes from? Do we associate Elgar with the Malverns because we know he lived there or because the music springs from the sights and sounds of that place? Elgar thought the latter. On his death bed he was whistling, rather feebly, a theme from the Concerto and said to a friend at his bedside, 'If ever you are walking the Malvern Hills and hear this – it's only me – don't be frightened.'

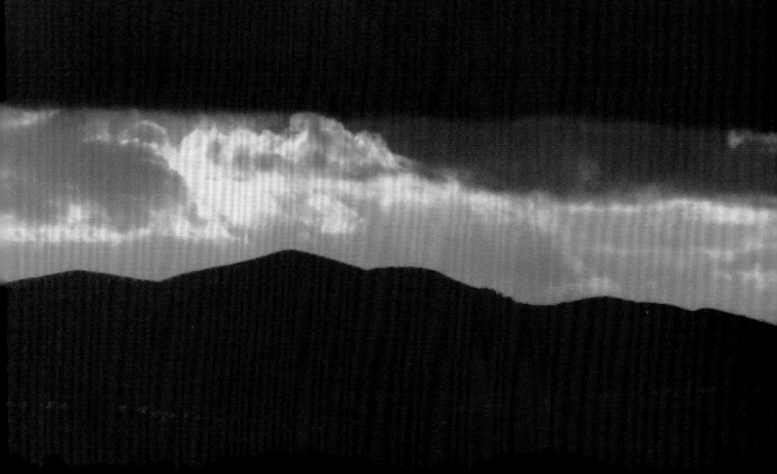

Paradise and Pandemonium

RICHARD HUMPHREYS

Upon the midlands now the industrious muse doth fall,
The shires which we the heart of England well may call.

MICHAEL DRAYTON, *Poly-Olbion* 1622

The 'Heart of England' suggests the industrial regions of the West and East Midlands, centred on cities such as Birmingham and Derby and their surrounding landscapes, which provided much of the energy and raw materials for their manufacturing activities, and which together are associated with England's power as a nation. Another 'Heart of England' exists, however: the area around the Cotswolds Hills and, further afield, with the rural districts between Worcester, Northampton and Oxford. This area is powerfully evoked by Edward Thomas's famous poem 'Adelstrop', which brings a steam train to rest in a timeless and remote Cotswolds village during the summer of 1914.

> Yes, I remember Adelstrop –
> The name, because one afternoon
> Of heat the express-train drew up there
> Unwontedly. It was late June.
>
> The steam hissed. Someone cleared his throat.
> No one left and no one came
> On the bare platform. What I saw
> Was Adelstrop –
> only the name
>
> And willows, willow-herb, and grass,
> And meadowsweet, and haycocks dry,
> No whit less still and lonely fair
> Than the high cloudlets in the sky.
>
> And for that minute a blackbird sang
> Close by, and round him, mistier,
> Farther and farther, all the birds
> Of Oxfordshire and Gloucestershire.

E. THOMAS, *Adelstrop* 1914

Joseph Wright of Derby (1734–1797),
An Iron Forge Viewed from Without
1773 (detail)

George Stubbs (1724–1806), *Horse Frightened by a Lion* ?exhibited 1763

When George Eliot, a great interpreter of the 'Heart of England', quoted the lines from Drayton's poem at the start of her novel *Felix Holt* in 1866, she was acknowledging the many resonances of the phrase. By the time Edward Thomas used it as the title of his celebrated book about the English countryside in 1906, it was understood to convey a more general sense of something beyond place and even time. The book begins in the grey streets of London, which resemble a 'great storehouse where yards of goods, all of one pattern, are exposed, all with that painful lack of character that makes us wish to rescue one and take it away and wear it, and soil it, and humanize it rapidly'. Within a few pages he escapes, by train, to the land of Richard the Ploughman and 'the wide prospect . . . and the dawn – the green hedges starred with white stitchwort flower, misty with the first hawthorn clusters, a-flutter with white-throat, wild with the warbling of the black-cap in their depths; wide, lustrous meadows dimmed by cuckoo-flowers, and at the edges of them the oaks beginning to bud and their branches like great black brands about to break into golden flame.' He moves from the world of modern labour to that of ancient toil, from prose to poetry, from greyness to colour, from death to life: from pandemonium to paradise.

Samuel Hieronymous Grimm (1733–1794), *Cresswell Crags, Derbyshire* 1785

THE WONDERS OF DERBYSHIRE

Creswell Crags lie on the Nottinghamshire–Derbyshire border in 'Robin Hood Country', and comprise a network of caves and fissures around a deep magnesium limestone gorge that runs along the Wellow Valley. The caves, with names such as 'Church Hole' and 'The Pin Hole', have been known for centuries for their remains of pre-historic animals and other archaeological curiosities. Since 1874 they have been systematically excavated and in 2003 Palaeolithic etchings were discovered deep inside one of them, establishing the area as an important heritage site. When George Stubbs painted Creswell Crags in the 1760s he would almost certainly have known about their associations with ancient British history, although these were then unfamiliar to the many tourists following the popular itineraries of the time. The intrepid Stubbs claimed to have painted the cliffs 'on the spot' for a series of hunting paintings, and they can be recognised as the location for a number of his works that depict horses, leopards, cheetahs and stags. By the time the nineteenth-century excavations began, the caves were known to include the remains of bison, woolly rhinos, horses and cave lions, the latter two the subject of a series that Stubbs painted in about 1763.

Horse Frightened by a Lion, exhibited at the Society of Artists in London in 1763, is the first in a series of Stubbs's works that can be understood as 'wildlife history paintings'. Inspired by a famous classical sculpture, Stubbs shows in this painting a horse rearing up as a lion leaves its cave nearby. The subsequent three episodes show the lion attacking and then finally devouring the noble but helpless horse. Stubbs paints recognisable parts of Creswell Crags as the dramatic primeval setting for his narrative of animal instinct and passion. Stubbs's choice of setting betrays more than his personal interest in the area. Britain's historic past was increasingly of interest to antiquaries, archaeologists, artists and tourists.

A few miles to the west of Creswell Crags lies the Peak District. This was certainly on the tourist's itinerary by the second half of the eighteenth century, on account of the writer William Gilpin's warm recommendation to travellers of the Derbyshire town of Matlock and the valleys of the Derwent and the Dove to the south. His claim that 'every object . . . is sublime, and wonderful' encouraged huge numbers of visitors to the area each year. Much of the attraction of the Peaks, close to the growing regional centres such as Sheffield and the fashionable spa town of Buxton, lay in its combination of natural beauty and the strangeness of its geological forms of millstone grit and limestone. This was a new world for tourists, which offered spectacular rivers and caves suggestive of some primitive past, while also being the setting of the Duke of Devonshire's magnificent home at Chatsworth and the new industrial activities of mining and porcelain manufacture. Although Defoe had, early in the eighteenth century, derided the 'Wonderless Wonders of the Peak' as a 'houling wilderness', many travellers became fascinated by the area. One of its chief attractions was Peak's Hole at Castleton, also known as 'the Devil's Arse', the subject of a fantasy pantomime *The Wonders of Derbyshire*, by the artist Philip James de Loutherbourg, performed at Drury Lane Theatre in 1779.

This project is fascinating for the light it throws on the taste for British landscape sights at the time. So popular was the nation's scenery that London crowds now regarded their own landscape as on equal terms with traditionally admired continental sites. Those who made their way to the

Joseph Wright of Derby (1734–1797), *Matlock Tor by Daylight* mid–1780s

Joseph Wright's painting *Matlock Tor by Daylight* shows him catering to the new passion for the Peak District, combining natural science, through his accurate depiction of the rock formation and specific light effects, with a strong classical taste.

Peak District could return with pieces of local 'Blue John' rock, either roughly hewn or made into vases and other trinkets by a poor local population dependent on this passing trade. A magical little maquette by de Loutherbourg for *The Wonders of Derbyshire* shows the shacks of a small community of such people, who would also offer candle-lit guided tours grounded in local legend, dressed in a 'picturesque' ragged garb and speaking with an authentic local accent. One traveller, the antiquary William Bray, recorded his two-hour tour of Peak's Hole, with its deep Styx-like streams and low rock ceiling that opens to a great height, describing the discomfort of the slow movement by boat and being carried upon the guide's back. A Mrs Murray gave advice for ladies about what to wear, recommending a 'night cap' to protect against the dripping from the roof of the cave and old gloves with which to hold a candle, as well as snuff and tobacco for the 'old witch-looking beings, spinning in the dark mouth of the cave'. Another visitor describes the haunting, echoing song of an unearthly and ragged local choir, whose 'discordant tones and wild appearances harmonized with the rugged rocks and inscrutable darkness'. Here was 'sublimity' on a grand scale, an 'abode of silent horror', that evokes an ancient civilisation where man and nature are imagined to have existed in some strange concordance. 'The mind, overpowered sometimes shrinks within itself, but as others rise to the sublime conception of the power that tore the rock asunder', wrote an Oxford man as he imagined the cave being the den of *banditti* and restless spirits and his guide a 'nocturnal villain, skulking from the avengers of murder'.

An artistic contemporary and acquaintance of Stubbs and de Louther-bourg was Joseph Wright 'of Derby'. His painting *Matlock Tor by Daylight* of the mid-1780s shows him catering to the new passion for the Peak District, combining natural science, through his accurate depiction of the rock formation and specific light effects, with a strong classical taste. Wright was part of a thriving Midlands culture of scientists, inventors, industrialists, writers and artists dedicated to harnessing new knowledge and mechanical power to the growth of Britain.

Joseph Wright of Derby (1734–1797), *Sir Brooke Boothby* 1781

Arkwright's Cotton Mills by Night is not only a realistic depiction of a factory building ablaze with light in the early hours of the morning, but also a meditation on natural and man-made power.

Joseph Wright of Derby (1734–1797), *Arkwright's Cotton Mills by Night c.*1782–3

One such figure was Sir Brooke Boothby, a Derbyshire landowner and member of the Lichfield literary circle, whom Wright painted in 1781. He is shown by Wright reclining by a stream, in what appears to be the Derbyshire landscape, holding a copy of *Rousseau, Juge de Jean Jacques*, which he had edited the year before and was written by his friend the Swiss philosopher Jean Jacques Rousseau. Boothby had met Rousseau in the 1760s during the latter's exile in England, when his revolutionary ideas about children's education and the power of nature had made him a fashionable mentor for many intellectuals such as Erasmus Darwin, Wright and the Cambridge botanist Thomas Martyn. Thus Boothby poses as 'a man of feeling', to quote the title of Henry Mackenzie's popular novel of 1771 based on Rousseau's ideas, wearing plain, simple clothes and reflecting on the joys of communing with nature. In this sense he is a precursor of the Romantic figure in the landscape that we find in William Wordsworth's poetry.

Wright is perhaps best known, however, for his dramatically lit scenes of scientific investigation and the early Industrial Revolution that took place in the depths of his native landscape. The gothic scene *Arkwright's Cotton Mills by Night* is not only a realistic depiction of a new factory building ablaze with light in the early hours of the morning, but also a meditation on natural and man-made power. The mills were a tourist attraction, especially at night, and evoked for many visitors a mixture of awe and admiration, horror and national pride. The aristocrat John Byng wrote in

1790 that they reminded him, standing on the banks of the River Derwent, of a 'first rate man of war' as well as looking 'most luminously beautiful'.

The spinning frame that lay at the heart of Richard Arkwright's industrial empire, was driven by water power. A key fascination for artist and tourist in central England at this time was the natural power residing in the landscape, be it aquatic or mineral. The belief that modernisation was part of nature's order was an important component of contemporary faith in the inevitability and moral importance of Britain's industrial growth. In this view, shared by many, there existed an unbroken line connecting the deep secrets of the nation's primitive past, visible at Creswell Crags and Peak's Hole, with the idealised notion of the country's future; the question of Britain's destiny, quite literally, lay in the soil. Many of Wright's patrons were local. John Whitehurst was a Derbyshire geologist who had found evidence of the county's volcanic origins in the interleaving of toadstone and limestone at Matlock Tor, which encouraged some to describe Switzerland as the 'Derbyshire of Europe'. His friend Peter Perez Burdett was the first precise cartographer of Derbyshire, whose map of his home county showed major routes 'for the ease and advancement of the national commerce' as well as forges, mines and a detailed plan of Derby as a cross-

...while red the countless fires,
With umber'd flames,
bicker on all thy hills,
Dark'ning the Summer's sun
with columns large
Of thick, sulphureous smoke
ANNA SEWARD, 'Colebrook Dale'

Joseph Wright of Derby (1734–1797), *An Iron Forge Viewed from Without* 1773

Philip James de Loutherbourg (1740–1812), *Coalbrookdale by Night* 1801

roads of economic and commercial activity. For his patron John Sargent, Wright made detailed plans to illustrate his alchemical poem of scientific enlightenment, 'The Mine' (1785), which incorporated Whitehurst's ideas.

Wright's *Iron Forge Viewed from Without* is one of a number of paintings of the iron-working that was taking place in the Derbyshire landscape. We are shown a ruined building standing by the banks of the River Derwent, all in a moonlit landscape. Behind the building are cliffs, with the wood and limestone required for smelting. At the heart of the painting a man with his back to us holds an iron bar on an anvil, while an ironmaster looks on. The water-powered tilt-hammer beyond him is about to beat the bar into an ingot of cast iron as the revolving drum turns. Watching this latter-day Vulcan's forge is a family group: a mother holding a baby and a dishevelled middle-aged man. The whole effect is complex: we are witnessing a scene familiar to Wright's contemporaries, yet the manner in which the artist portrays it seems to imbue this everyday event with religious significance.

THE NEW IRON AGE

By the end of the eighteenth century Britain was a country radically transformed from its agricultural condition of only fifty years before. Wright's friend de Loutherbourg's *Coalbrookdale at Night* of 1801 is the most famous image of this extraordinary new world. By the time it was painted, Coalbrookdale in Shropshire was not only a major centre of coke-based ironworking and pottery manufacture, but also a tourist attraction in its own right. Abraham Darby's 1779 Iron Bridge across the Severn was a cast-iron masterpiece. Spanning over one hundred feet and rising forty-five feet above the gorge, it was hailed for its harmonious relationship with its picturesque setting. One ironmaster boasted in a prospectus that 'there are perhaps few places where rural prospects and scenes of hurry and Business are so happily united as at Coalbrookdale'.

De Loutherbourg's painting has a melodramatic infernal quality, which reflects the feelings of wonder and horror experienced by tourists of the Picturesque, who would often stop by on their way to or from Wales. De Loutherbourg, as we have seen, was a theatrical designer and this work demonstrates his brilliant dramatic imagination. On returning from a sketching tour of Wales, his attention was attracted by the forges, mills and kilns lying along the banks of the Severn, with their smoke-belching chimneys and the yellow glare of the blast furnaces that transformed iron ore into the metal that became synonymous with the Industrial Revolution. Moon and fire compete to illuminate the smoky red scene with its heroic figures who struggle through the landscape littered with the huge forms of iron pipes and other macabre shapes. By 1800 what had only a few years earlier been seen as a heroic progress towards enlightenment in the 'Workshop of the World', was now being viewed as a true 'Pandemonium'.

The Lichfield poet Anna Seward was one of the first to sound a warning note about this sublime landscape in her poem 'Colebrook Dale' of 1785. She mourns the flight of the old natural spirits such as the 'wood-nymphs' from their rightful domain:

> Now we view
> Their fresh, their fragrant, and their silent reign
> Usurpt by Cyclops; – hear, in mingled tones,
> Shout their throng'd barge, their pond'rous engines clang
> Through thy coy dales; while red the countless fires,

John Rose & Co., commemorative mug with view of Ironbridge, c.1800–20

Abraham Darby's 1779 Iron Bridge across the Severn was a cast-iron masterpiece. Spanning over one hundred feet and rising forty-five feet above the gorge, it was hailed for its harmonious relationship with its picturesque setting.

William Williams (1758–1797), *View of Ironbridge* 1780

> With umber'd flames, bicker on all thy hills,
> Dark'ning the Summer's sun with columns large
> Of thick, sulphureous smoke, which spread, like palls,
> That screen the dead, upon the Sylvan robe
> Of thy aspiring rocks; pollute thy gales,
> And stain thy glassy waters.

The spread of industrial sites across the landscape of rural Britain, with their new technologies, townships, canals and increasing social and environmental problems, was matched from 1830 by the growth of the railway network. This was again quickly perceived to be both a benefit and a problem for society and attracted the interest of artists such as J.M.W. Turner and writers including Thomas Carlyle and Wordsworth. Fears about the damage being done to the physical and social landscape were set against admiration for man's ingenuity and the new pleasures of speedy travel through that landscape. Wordsworth's sonnet 'Steamboats, Viaducts and Railways' of 1833 gives some flavour of the response:

> Motions and Means, on land and sea at war
> With old poetic feeling, not for this,
> Shall ye, by Poets even, be judged amiss!
> Nor shall your presence, howso'er it mar
> The loveliness of Nature, prove a bar

To the Mind's gaining that prophetic sense
Of future change, that point of vision, whence
May be discovered what in soul ye are.
In spite of all that beauty may disown
In your harsh features, Nature doth embrace
Her lawful offspring in Man's art; and Time,
Pleased with your triumphs o'er his brother Space,
Accepts from your bold hands the proffered crown
Of hope, and smiles on you with cheer sublime.

David Cox was born in Birmingham, the son of an ironsmith. He
painted three versions of a moonlit view across the Midlands landscape
of the Birmingham–Liverpool express. He contrasts a frightened horse,
representing the natural world, with the distant blazing fire of the train
speeding across the land – an image of man's mechanical power. Like de

Monsal Viaduct, Derbyshire

David Cox (1783–1859), *The Night Train* c.1849

Loutherbourg, Cox was trained as a theatrical designer and he evokes a mythical scene in which past and present are seen in dramatic conflict. The 1865 poem 'The Night Express' by the civil servant William Cosmo Monkhouse closely echoes the spirit of the painting:

> Now – through the level plain,
> While, like a mighty mane,
> Stretches my endless breath in cloudy miles;
> Now – o'er a dull lagoon,
> While the broad beamed moon
> Lights up its sadness into sickly smiles.

J.C. Bourne, in contrast to Cox, describes in loving detail the new machines and the extraordinary forms of engineering they demanded in the forms of tunnels, viaducts, sheds and embankments. He produced wash drawings and lithographs for the engraved portfolios *London and Birmingham Railway* (1839) and *Great Western Railway* (1846). Engineers and designers such as Robert Stephenson and Isambard Kingdom Brunel became the heroes of the period. Bourne's work was sponsored by the antiquary and

J.C. Bourne (1773–1854), 'Kilsby Tunnel', from *Drawings of the London and Birmingham Railway* 1839

enthusiast for industrial growth, John Britton, who saw it as perfect visual propaganda to encourage Parliament to support the new railways. The artist himself believed that they would 'gratify both the lover of the Picturesque and the man of science'. This was at odds with Gilpin's view that in works of beauty 'the arts of industry are rejected', but Bourne found order where others, such as Charles Dickens, saw only confusion. In fact he found few buyers for his portfolios and discovered that although some engineers and businessmen might be enthusiastic, art collectors in general were little interested in the forces changing the landscape.

The Great Exhibition of 1851, held in Joseph Paxton's huge iron and glass 'Crystal Palace' in London's Hyde Park, brought much of the growing debate about the 'condition of England' to a head as a total of six million visitors flocked to see it from around the world. This ambitious project initiated by Prince Albert and Henry Cole was the first-ever international exhibition of manufactured goods, inventions, art and design. Unsurprisingly, the exhibition, intended to celebrate British art and society, provoked a great deal of controversy. Much of the design was from the Midlands and was seen as vulgar and unoriginal. The condition of those working in the factories and furnaces that produced these goods also concerned many observers, including Friedrich Engels and the social reformer Charles Booth. In addition, fears over the pollution and desecration of Britain's 'green and pleasant land' became ever more intense.

Over the hundred years that followed the exhibition it is reasonable to suggest that British artists turned increasingly to the countryside and its real or imagined virtues, and struggled to come to terms with the visual and imaginative possibilities of modernisation. Two artists with family

The Great Exhibition of 1851 was staged in Joseph Paxton's enormous Crystal Palace in London's Hyde Park. It had to be built around huge trees which could not be cut down for fear of a public outcry – a small victory for nature over machinery. W. Robert and Joseph Dickinson were important lithographers and publishers working in the mid-nineteenth century.

Dickinson Bros., *Waiting for the Queen* 1851

Edward Butler Bayliss (1874–1950), *Evening in the Black Country* c.1910

backgrounds in industrial England are among the few exceptions to this tendency: Edwin Butler Bayliss and Edward Wadsworth. Both painted Black Country landscapes, though from entirely different artistic perspectives.

Bayliss, the son of a Wolverhampton iron-founder, left the family firm at the beginning of the twentieth century to work as a self-taught artist. His main subject was the industrial landscape in the Bilston and Tipton area, especially near the Hickman steelworks owned by a family friend. He painted dark figures moving slowly through the ravaged and smog-bound landscape, over which pitheads, blast furnaces and chimneys tower. A reviewer in 1911 described Bayliss as 'the poet-painter of the industrial scarred country around Wolverhampton' with its 'smoke-charged atmosphere'.

Wadsworth, by contrast, was a modernist. The son of a wealthy Bradford cotton manufacturer, he trained as an engineer and draughtsman before becoming a painter. A central figure in the avant-garde Vorticist movement, which pioneered a semi-abstract art drawing on industrial imagery, he later became a war artist. After the war he turned his attention to the landscape of the Black Country. The result is a series of woodcuts and drawings that, although unsentimental like Bayliss's works, go much further in their interpretation of the scenery (see p.120). Stark and uncompromising, they also suggest some primeval power behind the chimneys and slag heaps, which is reminiscent of the more optimistic vision of Wright and other early painters of modernisation. Wadsworth saw artistic possibilities in the seeming battlefields of Netherton and Tipton, which were lost on most contemporaries.

Since the 1850s, and the rise of Pre-Raphaelitism as well as the spread of
the ideas of the art critic John Ruskin, a new fascination with the natural
world was in the ascendant. It was religious in inspiration and sought to
reinvent a traditional relationship between man and nature. One artist
who embodied this fresh covenant with God's creation was the Catholic
painter John Rogers Herbert. His *Laborare est Orare* (To Work is to Pray)
of 1862 shows Cistercian monks labouring in the sunny stone-walled
fields near their monastery in Leicestershire. This had been designed by
the Catholic architect and designer Augustus Pugin in the 1840s, and was
the first monastery to have been built since the Reformation, following
the emancipation of English Catholics in 1829. The revival of Catholic
worship, since the emergence of the High Church Oxford Movement
in the 1830s, had made a considerable impression on many artists. Not
only was there a sense of artistic and spiritual renewal, there was also a
corresponding sense of the dangers of a Protestant culture that had lost
its sense of values, and which had been responsible for the destruction of
a medieval culture it had subsequently failed to emulate. Herbert, who can
be seen in the foreground piously drawing this true 'Heart of England',
shows monks who seem to have stepped out of a medieval book of hours,
harvesting the crop and living according to the seasons and a god-given rule.

John Rogers Herbert (1810–1890), *Laborare est Orare* 1862

William Morris's home at Kelmscott, Gloucestershire

Forget six counties overhung with smoke,
Forget the smarting steam and piston stroke,
Forget the spreading of the hideous town;
Think rather of the pack-horse on the down,
And dream of London, small and white and clean,
The clear Thames bordered by its gardens green.
WILLIAM MORRIS from *The Earthly Paradise* (1868–70)

To the right a poor girl is offered a loaf of bread. Here is a prescription for a reformation of Britain in rural fields away from the despoiled cities and exploitative factories.

Further south, the designer and writer William Morris had moved with his wife Jane to the Red House near Bexleyheath in Kent in 1860. Designed by Philip Webb to Morris's specifications, the red brick building with its mix of medieval and modern forms, chivalric frescoes and richly planted gardens, was the first of his efforts to create an ideal home. Through the products of his firm Morris, Marshall and Faulkner and Co., Morris sought to transform people's homes and lives with new forms of fabric, tile, furniture and wallpaper design based on simple, natural and medieval patterns. These were the direct antithesis of the goods displayed at Crystal Palace and a challenge to the High Victorian 'kitsch' of Coalbrookdale. They proposed not just a new style, but a new social order.

In 1871 Morris moved to Kelmscott Manor, near Lechlade in Gloucestershire, on the eastern edge of the Cotswolds, sharing a tenancy with the painter Dante Gabriel Rossetti. Morris believed in what the title of

Broadway, Worcestershire

one of his books described as 'The Earthly Paradise' and while creating a new ideal home at Kelmscott wrote on social justice, joined the Social Democratic Federation and founded the Society for the Protection of Ancient Buildings. His hugely influential novel *News From Nowhere* (1890) describes an English utopia of the future. Morris's move presaged a considerable exodus of artists, designers, writers and idealists from the cities to the Cotswolds in the later nineteenth century, 'a mystery land', as he wrote, 'of difficult hills and deeply wooded valleys'.

Ironically, the first notable artistic appearances in the area, which was blighted by the 1870s agricultural depression and therefore contained cheap properties, were Americans who had a love of English vernacular country architecture and the money to buy it. The New England painter Francis Davis Millet settled in Broadway, Worcestershire, during 1884 on the advice of Morris. Millet's lovingly restored old properties in the village became the perfect backdrop for his paintings of seventeenth-century English history and the area as a whole had what his friend, the novelist Henry James, called 'the perfection of the old English rural tradition'.

Friends soon came to stay in Broadway to enjoy the musky, candle-lit interiors and summer landscape, including the literary illustrator Edwin

John Singer Sargent working at
Fladbury, 1889

John Singer Sargent (1856–1925), *Lady Fishing –
Mrs Ormond* 1889

Austin Abbey, the writer Robert Louis Stevenson and the painters Alfred
Parsons and John Singer Sargent. Henry James believed that in Broadway
Millet had 'reconstructed the Golden Age', with the annual celebration of
haymaking, intermittent alfresco eating, boating, tennis parties, musical
concerts and poetry readings. 'The place has so much character', he wrote,
'it rubs off', perhaps unaware that the local population was perplexed by
the loud, new and cosmopolitan arrivals. The response they received was
often dour: 'Them Americans is out again'.

Sargent, recently arrived from Paris in 1884, spent a number of summers with the Millets to whose circle he was introduced by James. It was at Russell House, their main residence, that he painted his celebrated *Carnation, Lily, Lily, Rose* of 1885–6, drawing in part on the imagery of innocence in Stevenson's popular 'A Child's Garden of Verse', written at Broadway in 1885. In the summer of 1889 Sargent rented the rectory house in Fladbury, on the River Avon in the Vale of Evesham, just north of Broadway, which also became a haunt for artists and friends escaping city life. His unfinished *Lady Fishing – Mrs Ormond* shows his sister Violet by the river, the fishing pole she was holding left unpainted. It is one of a number of summer scenes of leisurely life on the river in which Sargent recreates the atmosphere of classic Impressionist painting. Like his French mentors, Sargent evokes the transitory pleasures of a rural idyll in a fast-moving modern world dominated by the dissipating forces of the city and industrialisation. It was, of course, an idyll entirely dependent on that modern world and its economic and cultural life.

Henry James, as T. S. Eliot said, 'was possessed by the vision of an ideal society'. But, like many who visited Broadway, he had a vision of 'Merrie England', in his case that of the romantic *nouveau-riche* exile searching for roots and authenticity. Other, more indigenous, searchers after paradise in the Cotswolds sought a radically new life, drawing not only on local culture and materials but also on ideals of life, work and leisure that did not require the backing of an international bank account. The anti-capitalist theories of Morris, with their ideal of a 'democracy of art', supplied a generation of artists and designers with a dream of a new world. This world, based on egalitarian principles, would provide functional art as opposed to frivolous decoration, manual work as opposed to machine production and a genuine love of the natural world rather than of eclectic fantasy. The architect and designer Charles Ashbee's Guild of Handicraft, founded in London's East End, moved 'in toto' to Chipping Campden in 1902. Dedicated to the idea of 'standard' and self-consciously 'English' in its character, it constituted the most serious effort to realise this vision in which the modern distinctions between art, life and work would disappear in a setting unscathed by John Ruskin's mechanised 'storm cloud'. Books such as J. Arthur Gibbs's *A Cotswold Village* (1898) were among many that painted a pastoral Eden where England could reinvent itself through the revival of good, honest craftsmanship and a religious re-connection with the 'spirit of the land'.

F.L. Griggs (1876–1938), *Duntisbourne Rouse* 1927

William Rothenstein (1872–1945), *Barn at Cherington, Gloucestershire* 1935

Tellingly, the 1890s also saw the founding of the National Trust, which spread the gospel of the new 'back to the land' movement to a wider public.

The topographical and architectural artist F.L. Griggs moved to Chipping Campden in 1904, following a tour to make drawings for his illustrations to *Oxford and the Cotswolds* as part of Macmillan's famous *Highways and Byways* series. Griggs, a disciple of Ruskin and admirer of Samuel Palmer's pastoral prints, exhibited with the struggling Cotswold-based Guild of Craftsmen and made drawings of local buildings for Ashbee. By 1912 Griggs had converted to Roman Catholicism, 'that Ancient Faith of England', as he called it. It was a logical move for a man in love with a Gothic past and fearful of 'the passing of the Old & the coming of the terrible New in the Cotswolds'. Like many during this period, from Vaughan Williams who 'rediscovered' English folk song and Cecil Sharp who did the same for folk dance, he sought ancient certainties in a world that seemed to be running out of control. He was later an executive member of the campaigning Council for the Preservation of Rural England.

In his etchings Griggs sought an intense spiritual immersion in the land and buildings of 'old England', revealing his anguished sense of loss in the title of one print, *Ex Anglia Perdita* of 1921. The densely worked shadows, bursts of evidently divine light and rich textures of stone and foliage are an expression of the almost painful feelings about which he wrote to his friend Russell George Alexander: 'Think of dear old Samuel Palmer (who ought to have been a Catholic, & wasn't so far away) think of the Country, the Sky, & the Seasons. Pastoral imagery, & how it's derived mainly from Scriptures, & what is there more beautiful?' *Duntisbourne Rouse* (1927), with its crescent moon, rooks and sheep, is an elegiac image in the tradition of Palmer dedicated to the memory of his friend, Ernest Gimson, who had married in the ancient Cotswolds chapel depicted. Griggs, who in 1921 designed a logo for his dealer Hilda Finberg's popular Cotswold Gallery in London, later had a major impact on young artists as a teacher at the Royal College of Art in the 1920s, including Graham Sutherland who also converted to Catholicism.

The 1920s and 1930s saw many artists moving to or spending much time in an area that was now securely part of the modern Picturesque tourist's itinerary, with its well-trodden footpaths and motored lanes. Major architects and designers such as Norman Jewson, Ernest Gimson and Alfred and Louise Powell lived and worked in the Cotswolds in the early twentieth century and would have been among the attractions for an artist such as William Rothenstein who bought the Jewson-renovated Iles Farm at Far Oakridge in 1914 as a summer dwelling. Rothenstein commissioned local craftsmen to make work for his home, including an enormous painted cupboard built in around 1914 by Gimson and decorated with Cotswolds landscape scenes by Powell, and a Wedgwood earthenware punch bowl painted with views of Gloucestershire by Powell in 1928. Rothenstein, who entertained a host of visitors to Iles Farm such as W. B. Yeats and John Galsworthy, continued to refer to his home as 'spiritually Cotswolds' even after he had sold the house.

By the 1930s, though, the heyday of Cotswolds idealism was over and the area was even alluded to humorously in popular books such as E. F. Benson's 'Mapp and Lucia' novels. Broadway and Chipping Camden were visited by thousands of tourists each year. During and after the inter-war period, many artists, including Stanley and Gilbert Spencer, Stanley Badmin and James Bateman, painted often luxuriant images of a fecund and re-enchanted Cotswolds, helping to establish it as the classic 'Heart of England' landscape.

T. S. Eliot's famous poem 'The Wasteland' (1922) shared many of those concerns about the industrialised world that we saw in Edward Thomas's writing at the start of this chapter. Like many before him, he found some certainty in a world of change by becoming a Christian and extolling the virtues of a lost pastoral world. Following in the footsteps of fellow

Alfred Powell (1865–1960), *Punch Bowl with views of Gloucestershire* 1928

James Bateman (1893–1959), *Haytime in the Cotswolds* 1939

Americans such as John Singer Sargent and Henry James, he became
passionate about the Cotswolds in the 1920s and 1930s and in 1927 was
baptised at the church in Finstock, an idyllic village in Wychwood Forest.
His *Four Quartets* includes the poem 'Burnt Norton', a title taken from
the name of an old manor house near Chipping Campden. He evokes
the timeless presence lost since the days of Joseph Wright:

> Time past and time future
> Allow but a little consciousness.
> To be conscious is not to be in time
> But only in time can the moment in the rose-garden,
> The moment in the arbour where the rain beat,
> The moment in the draughty church at smokefall
> Be remembered; involved with past and future.
> Only through time time is conquered.

The Flatlands

You know when you have reached East Anglia and the Fens: your eyes are drawn not down to the landscape but up to the sky. Of all the parts of Britain this is the place with the grandest skyscapes, a flat land with a huge dome above it of ever-changing shapes, at its best on a summer day when rounded white cumulus piles high up on itself leaving glimpses of blue that seem to stretch to infinity. It is a place that has to be visited for its own sake because it is not on the way to anywhere. Even today when the grand city of Norwich boasts high-tech service industries the main road shrinks from a motorway to a dual carriageway and finally to the original simple main road. Local people sometimes grumble about their poor communications with the rest of Britain, but I think they also relish it too. Because East Anglia is a place set apart, even a little introverted. Many years ago I worked for a local television programme there, and I remember the most popular item was not the news we brought from the modern world but a farmer leaning over a five-barred gate telling folk stories in local dialect.

Everything here is movement. If it is not the sky, it is water, not just the sea but the water inland, the dykes and the Broads. Travelling by train from London to the North East you pass through an area of flat land where the soil darkens almost to black, criss-crossed by thin strips of silver water. This is the western edge of the Fens, land either reclaimed from the sea or holding the sea at bay. At Dunwich on the Suffolk coast is a vivid reminder of what happens when the sea wins – the old sea port has now fallen beneath the waves, except for the remains of a Franciscan friary poised on the cliff edge. It is said that, like Debussy's *La Cathedrale Engloutie*, you can still hear the bells ringing out from the church tower. Turner's magnificent watercolour with a huge wave threatening the village suggests a place buried with all its secret horrors under the sea.

Inland, near Grantham, is a tiny hamlet which I have only visited once. It is called Dembleby and is where my family name comes from. It is in the area of Lincolnshire called Holland – a reminder of the close

"Of all the parts of Britain this is the place with the grandest skyscapes, a flat land with a huge dome above it of ever-changing shapes, at its best on a summer day"

Dedham Vale

George Stubbs (1724–1806), *Otho, with John Larkin Up* 1768

links with the country which played such an important part in the history of East Anglia and the development of the dazzling landscape painting which became the supreme form of English art.

Everywhere you go in this shyly seductive countryside you come across reminders of the prosperity it once enjoyed. There are fine cathedrals and hundreds of equally fine churches whose spires you can see from miles away reaching up out of the flat land to the heavens.

That prosperity was closely tied to Holland itself, which had a long history of trade across the North Sea. It was the Dutch whose skills were used over four hundred years ago to drain the fens and manage the Broads. And with their trade came merchants, some of whom settled, bringing with them the work of their artists. So it is not surprising that when Gainsborough and Constable after him started painting landscape they should look to the Dutch example: the same huge skies and a landscape defined by water. But they were not alone. A school of painting in Norwich whose leading lights were John Sell Cotman and John Crome also found their inspiration from earlier Dutch landscape artists. Crome was even known as 'the Norfolk Hobbema'. Dutch painting had established a tradition of recording sea and landscape when the rest of Europe and Britain was engrossed in figure painting, either religious or classical. In Holland the Protestant revolution helped to legitimise landscape as God's work and therefore deemed it worthy of artists' attention. It was this work

Tidal Marshes near the junction of the rivers
Waveny and Yare, Norfolk Broads

Potato crops in a field near Happisburgh, Norfolk

which the Norfolk painters had seen and admired and which makes East Anglia so pivotal in the history of our understanding of landscape.

There is nothing derivative about these painters though. Everything comes from something and they developed the style of the Dutch masters and adapted it to their own country and their own distinct vision of it. Constable must rank in popular taste as the master of them all. *The Hay Wain* remains the most popular of all English landscape paintings, reproduced whenever an image of rustic tranquillity is needed,

though that simple interpretation diminishes the picture's impact. As with so many of Constable's paintings, the reality is complex and demands careful study. I have always found his drawings and watercolour sketches more accessible, but then that is true of almost any painter. The working drawings have a freshness and timelessness that can be lost in the formality of the finished work.

Constable has the rare distinction of being an artist who does not just embody a particular landscape but subsequently has that landscape embody him. In a rare example of

Cley Mill, Norfolk

John Crome (1768–1821), *Moonrise on the Yare c.*1811–16

nature imitating art the guardians of the countryside around Flatford Mill and Willy Lott's cottage now cut the trees and rushes to ensure the scene is as near as possible as Constable saw it. The same happened on a grander scale at Holkham Hall in Norfolk. Under the patronage of the great Norfolk grandee Thomas Coke, Earl of Leicester, William Kent created a garden according to the rules of landscape laid down by the French painter Claude Lorrain. There could be no place better suited to imposing the belief that man could improve on nature than this previously flat, windswept and treeless marsh. Even the views from some of the windows have been created to fit Claude's concept of the perfect classical landscape balanced in shape and tone.

No visit to East Anglia would be complete without a journey to Aldeburgh in Suffolk, the home of the composer Benjamin Britten. The strength of the sea, its remorseless attempt to eat up the land, a yard every year in East Anglia, has always had a powerful hold on artists's imaginations. Britten's portrait of the fisherman Peter Grimes, an embittered outcast from his village who eventually gives himself up to the sea, is full of the sounds of this coast, with interludes when you can hear the waves sucking at the shingle and the cries of birds overhead, the sea at dawn and during a mighty storm. Ralph Vaughan Williams, too, an essentially English composer to rank with Elgar, captured the same world in his *Norfolk Rhapsodies* and *In The Fen Country*.

Today Norfolk, Suffolk and Lincolnshire are still sufficiently their old selves to allow the visitor to go back in time and share the vision of these painters and musicians. Or perhaps just to wonder with Dickens's David Copperfield how: 'if the world were really as round as my geography book said, how any part of it came to be so flat'.

Aldeburgh beach

'The Nature of Our Looking'

DAVID BLAYNEY BROWN

In summer 2004, the same week as ramblers celebrated their new freedom of the Yorkshire Moors by setting out from Haworth Parsonage to roam in the footsteps of the Brontë sisters, a huge copy of John Constable's *Hay Wain* was created in London's Trafalgar Square in front of its home in the National Gallery. Assembled from sections painted by 150 different 'artists' including Constable's descendents (whose contributions were rushed to the capital under motorcycle escort), the copy was masterminded by Rolf Harris (whose own segment fell off) and filmed by the BBC. The press gushed statistics about the relative fame of Constable, the picture and Harris himself. *The Hay Wain* is the pictorial equivalent of Wordsworth's daffodils. So successful have Constable and his admirers been in persuading us that his vision was real and his art 'natural', that this scene on the Stour between

Copy of Constable's *The Hay Wain*, assembled from sections painted by 150 different contributors, summer 2004

OPPOSITE
John Constable (1776–1837),
Flatford Mill ('Scene on a Navigable River') 1816–17 (detail)

Suffolk and Essex, with a hay cart crossing the water and a farmhouse on its bank, has certainly become a Picture of Britain. If nature was discovered in the North, the East claimed naturalism as its own.

The first to recognise this were in fact the French, when Constable's picture was exhibited in Paris in 1824. It won a medal and impressed a new generation of landscape painters. Constable thought all this amusing, but not without irony. At home he remained a marginal figure, nowhere near the centre of the art world and a minority taste for his few admirers. Moreover East Anglia was a land apart, neither on the map of the 'Picturesque tour', nor thought to have any pictorial potential. It was an agricultural region, prosperous but workmanlike. Yet Constable was not alone in picturing what had once seemed unpromising subject matter. Thomas Gainsborough had painted in the Stour valley, a few miles to the

Richard Billingham (born 1970), *Untitled, Norfolk (Cows)* 2003

west of Constable, half a century earlier. Meanwhile, the Norwich School of painters, contemporaries of Constable, also created a distinctive landscape art. And yet in the art of Gainsborough and the Norwich painters a paradox arises. In the absence of any tradition of representing the East Anglian landscape, it was the earlier Dutch painters, whose work abounded in local collections, who showed them how to see it.

The Dutch painted their native dunes, heaths, meadows and rivers. Theirs was an art of parallel planes, of flatlands and huge skies – like East Anglia, in fact. At the reductive extreme of Richard Billingham's recent photographs, this is a landscape that, as Graham Swift has written in his novel *Waterland* (1983), 'approximates to Nothing'. It suits the pragmatic, empirical view of the Dutch painters whose countrymen had helped to form it. The presence of Dutch pictures was the result of a history of trade

Richard Billingham (born 1970), *Untitled, Norfolk (Dyke)* 2003

The Norwich artist George Vincent painted the annual 'Dutch fair', held on the shore at Yarmouth near the start of the fishing season.

George Vincent (1796–1832), *Dutch Fair on Yarmouth Beach* 1821

and contact across the North Sea. In the sixteenth and seventeenth centuries, Dutch engineers drained the Fens and managed the Norfolk Broads (whose larger wetlands had been the result of medieval peat diggings). In the eighteenth and nineteenth centuries, Dutch traders did business in Yarmouth and King's Lynn. The Norwich artist George Vincent painted the annual 'Dutch fair', held on the shore at Yarmouth near the start of the fishing season. Among Gainsborough's early patrons was Henry Muilman, one of a number of Dutch merchants and bankers who had set up business in the City of London and acquired estates east of the capital. Muilman's was at Dagenham, then open country. Gainsborough painted the merchant's son Peter and two friends from the Essex gentry in a landscape probably based equally on the area and on Dutch pictures belonging to the Muilmans.

CORNARD WOOD TO MOUSEHOLD HEATH

Somehow, around 1747, Gainsborough managed to draw a copy of Jacob van Ruisdael's picture known as '*La Forêt*' (1660–70). Gainsborough's exact source has never been identified, but in his most ambitious early landscape painting, *Cornard Wood* (*c.*1748), he showed how easily the Dutch painter's subject matter could be adapted to scenery around his native Sudbury. The rough, uneven ground, trees and undergrowth interspersed with winding tracks and standing water and set beneath a cloudy sky are all characteristic of Dutch painting. But here they are located to a particular place, a hillside at Abbas Hall, above Great Cornard, that looks south-west towards another village, Great Henny, whose church of St Mary's appears in the background. The 'unkempt' landscape and the activities of the numerous figures tell us that this was common land, used by the villagers, according to ancient rights, for grazing, digging marl for manure or sand for construction, or gathering firewood.

The topographical realism of Gainsborough's picture is striking if we know this area. So is its depiction of the current condition of the land. Gainsborough claimed he painted the picture in Sudbury in 1748. According to his friend Philip Thicknesse, 'there was not a Picturesque clump of Trees, no, nor hedge row, stone, or post . . . that he had not so perfectly in his mind's eye, that had he known he could use a pencil, he could have perfectly delineated'. More probably the picture was painted

Thomas Gainsborough (1727–1788), *'Gainsborough's Forest' (Cornard Wood)* c.1748

Thomas Hearne (1744–1817), *View in Suffolk* 1776

in London from these childhood impressions, together with what he described to a Norfolk friend as 'my first imitations of little Dutch landscapes'. *Cornard Wood* proved to be exceptional in uniting the styles of his favourite Dutch painters with a genuine naturalism based on his own experience. That parts of Suffolk really did look as wild as Gainsborough's wood is suggested by *View in Suffolk*, painted by the watercolourist Thomas Hearne in 1776. Hearne shows the area around Henstead in central Suffolk as common land, as yet largely unaffected by the process of enclosure, when land was literally fenced and placed under private management through Acts of Parliament. Later still in the century, John Robert Cozens found ploughed fields interspersed with slopes that remained wild and overgrown, near Langham, just across the Essex border in what would become 'Constable Country'.

Constable was critical of Gainsborough's later landscapes, regarding them as 'wide of nature'. But he greatly admired the early ones because he could see how they caught the free spirit of Suffolk; 'tis a most delightfull country for a landscape painter', he wrote in 1800 from Woodbridge, 'I fancy I see Gainsborough in every hedge and hollow tree.' By 1814, *Cornard Wood* belonged to his London-based uncle, David Pike Watts. That

John Crome's picture of a great oak at Poringland, a village south-east of Norwich, was sufficiently well-observed to be exhibited in 1824 as a 'Study from Nature'.

John Crome (1768–1821), *The Poringland Oak c.*1818–20

year, when exhibited in London at the British Institution, it was called simply 'A Woody Scene', and it has been suggested that Constable himself later recognised its subject. Gainsborough gave Constable roots, a local history to justify and encourage his own efforts. Neither painter felt the need to travel abroad. Of the Dutch painters he too admired, Constable commented that they were 'a stay at home people, hence their originality'. It was a view with which John Crome, the leading figure in the Norwich School, would surely have agreed. He visited London regularly and even went to Paris, but based himself in Norwich, where he was apprenticed to a coach and sign painter, and worked as a picture dealer, restorer and art teacher to local families. He eventually established an independent reputation as a painter and leading light in the Norwich Society of Artists.

Like Constable, Crome found his roots in Gainsborough and the Dutch. He copied both in local collections and his love of Dutch artists is apparent from his own pictures and prints, and from contemporary

John Crome (1768–1821), *Mousehold Heath, Norwich* c.1818–20

anecdotes. He was known as the 'Norfolk Hobbema', and according to his patron, Dawson Turner, would show off a new etching with the question 'What think you of this Ruysdael?' An interest in Dutch painting was by no means unusual at this period. However Crome, like the young Gainsborough, applied its lessons to his own locale. He could paint the backwaters of Norwich in the manner of Jan van Goyen or Adriaen van Ostade, or the moon rising over the river Yare like Rembrandt or Aert van der Neer, without any suspension of topographical belief. His picture of a great oak at Poringland, a village south-east of Norwich, was sufficiently well-observed to be exhibited in 1824 as a *Study from Nature*. At the same time, it pays tribute to the painters who had opened his eyes. The bright sky with its pink-tinged clouds comes from another Dutch artist, Aelbert Cuyp, while the composition concentrates *Cornard Wood* to a single, heroic motif. Crome passed through London several times in 1814 on his way to and from Paris, and must have seen Gainsborough's painting at the Institution.

One of the remarkable things about *Cornard Wood* is that it so accurately predicts the requirements of the Picturesque; yet it was not until 1794 that Uvedale Price's *Essays on the Picturesque* gave aesthetic credibility to the sort of random untidiness and wealth of foreground detail seen in the

Before the age of railroads, Norfolk and its capital city were outlying districts… wild, untrimmed, and picturesque.
RICHARD AND SAMUEL REDGRAVE, *A Century of British Painters*, 1866

John Crome (1768–1821), *The Steam Packet* c.1813–17

picture. Gainsborough painted them unconsciously, because he regarded them as true, both to the nature and the art that he was looking at. However, the relationship between such effects and the real condition of the land can never be taken for granted – even less so as they became part of aesthetic fashion and land itself became politically contentious. Crome's other great tribute to Cuyp, to Gainsborough and also to recent luminous landscapes and marines by J. M.W. Turner, is sufficient warning of this. *Mousehold Heath*, painted between 1818 and 1820, was probably one of his last major paintings and his most ambitious, depicting a subject close to the heart of his Norwich audience. Mousehold was a great open expanse stretching north-east of the city. The headquarters of Robert Kett's 'Norfolk Rebellion' against enclosure and other restrictions in 1549, it had been to Norwich what Cornard Wood was to Sudbury: common land for the free use of the local people. This is how Crome shows it, uncultivated, with haphazard tracks, its grass kept short by grazing and scattered with wild plants. But the reality was very different. The heath had been enclosed since 1799, fenced, gated and divided by new, straight roads.

Technically innovative in his art, Crome was not against progress. He painted the first steamer on the Yare, which carried passengers on what had been mainly a commercial waterway. But with *Mousehold Heath* his view was historical, as Gainsborough's at Cornard had not been. Although it happened to conform to picturesque ideals, his picture was probably not motivated by fashion or taste, but by social conviction that expressed itself in nostalgia. It asserted local tradition against national policy. Crome owned a copy of Nathaniel Kent's *General View of the Agriculture of the County of Norfolk* (1796), which argued for a modification of enclosure law to protect small farmers. Enclosure was only one of a succession of disruptive changes wrought on the landscape of East Anglia as elsewhere and reflected – or not – in its art. Crome was perhaps brave so conspicuously to ignore a development that enriched the proprietorial class who bought his work. His picture raised important questions for the landscape painter. How political can he be? How can pictorial values relate to the realities of land management? Who really owns the land? And what is the landscape painter's task – to record features or ways of life that might be disappearing, or to mark progress?

CONSTABLE AND CONSTABLE COUNTRY

Late in life, when he had long since moved away to London, Constable designed a series of prints that he called *English Landscape Scenery* (1830–2). The title might suggest a comprehensive set of views. But many were the Stour valley scenes that he said 'made me a painter'. The best description of the surrounding area of Dedham Vale is his own, recalling 'its gentle declivities, its luxuriant meadow flats sprinkled with flocks and herds, its well cultivated uplands, its woods and rivers, with numerous scattered villages and churches, farms and picturesque cottages'. This is exactly how it appears in the panorama he painted in 1800 for a local girl, Lucy Hurlock, who was marrying and moving to King's Lynn. This, like much of Constable's art, claimed to be a truthful witness. It was also a long goodbye.

Constable's father Golding Constable was an important figure in his area: a corn and coal merchant in East Bergholt with his own mills and barges, and a farmer too. Constable was expected to join the family business. He knew how the country worked as well as how it looked. His love of natural things fused with his enthusiasm for Gainsborough's early paintings and the Dutch, as we can see from a large portrait of a tree that he made at Helmingham in 1800. It was perhaps inevitable that Constable would become a realist or a naturalist. Or was it? An early mentor of Constable's was the artist and collector Sir George Beaumont, whose mother lived nearby at Dedham. Beaumont showed Constable his favourite picture by Claude – *Landscape with Hagar and the Angel* of 1646 (see p.11), now in the National Gallery – that he loved so much that it always travelled with him. Constable never forgot it. But he resisted the wider weight of art history, writing in 1802 to his friend John Dunthorne, the village plumber and glazier and also an amateur artist, that he was fed up with 'running after pictures and seeking the truth at second hand'; there was 'room enough for a natural painture'. He planned to attempt 'some laborious studies from nature' at Bergholt that summer, and 'a pure and unaffected representation of the scenes that may employ me'.

Naturalism, that defining movement in landscape art in the nineteenth century, had now found its voice. What of its expression? Hesitantly at first, Constable delivered on his promise to study outdoors. Since he was based in London from 1799, this was summer work, which he undertook in the lanes and fields overlooking the Stour or along the river itself.

John Constable (1776–1837), *The Mill Stream* c.1810

Constable took sketches like *The Mill Stream* of *c*.1810, which depicts the same house as in *The Hay Wain*, the home of a farmer called Willy Lott, back to London for reference. Several years later, he took a further step, painting, or at least beginning, pictures, before the motif. On such occasions, Lott's house was Constable's clock; when smoke rose from its chimney as the stove was lit for supper, he knew it was time to stop work. *Flatford Mill* was painted this way in the summer of 1816, and exhibited in London in 1817. It is a masterpiece of retrospect as well as realism. Constable associated his 'careless boyhood' with the Stour; it was picturesque, but also the source of his family's prosperity. Golding owned Flatford Mill, a watermill for grinding corn, and another mill at Dedham; his barges carried grain downstream for shipment to London, and coal and other imports upstream. *Flatford Mill* is sometimes seen as a farewell to Suffolk on the eve of the artist's marriage, but his father's death in 1816 was surely the central fact that dominated its conception. The view towards Golding's mill shows these barges that have passed one of his locks and are about to pass out of view under Flatford bridge. A boy on a towpath looks back towards them, echoing the painter's own metaphorical backward glance. On the towpath, a hat (Golding's?) lies abandoned. In a distant field a man with a scythe reminds us of Father Time or the grim reaper. Is it too fanciful to suggest yet another dimension to the picture: an echo, in the double perspective of winding river and stream, with which we know Constable took immense pains, of Gainsborough's *Cornard Wood*, which Constable's uncle had recently bought? The painting must have been discussed in the family and was, similarly, a summary of a Suffolk upbringing.

Constable's *Cornfield* of 1826, which hangs with *The Hay Wain* in the National Gallery, was another backward glance, and as definitive of its subject, an 'inland – cornfield – a close lane – kind of thing', as *Flatford Mill* had been of the river. By this time Constable was only an occasional visitor to Suffolk, so depended on recollections and earlier studies. For the picture he used a large oil sketch whose status – outdoor nature study or studio composition – is debated. If the former, it probably dates from 1817, his last Suffolk summer. In any event, the arrangement of vista and trees is reminiscent of Beaumont's Claude, and Constable turned the sketch into a picture about the past. The subject is Fen Lane, along which he used to walk to school. To suggest community in this pastoral land he added a village where there was none, and to mark his own presence in it, a boy drinking from a stream. Constable's sources were nature and Suffolk – both as important as his schoolroom lessons – which, like Wordsworth's daffodils, were stored in his memory to nourish his art. Constable transformed them by adding what he called 'eye-salve' to his picture, which some critics have regarded as too much of a gloss on reality or a concession to the taste of his London audience.

Tensions between naturalism and contrivance, past and present are not unique to Constable. He attracts them because he claimed to be a 'natural' painter, at a time when the pendulum of British life was swinging towards the city and agricultural practices were changing with unprecedented speed. He has been accused of ignoring this, of turning his back on mounting unrest among rural workers, even of assuming 'ownership' of the appearance of the Suffolk landscape just as his father or brother literally owned it ('the filthy fascist sod', as the late Bernard Levin declared in an ironic outburst in *The Times*). But the Suffolk 'peasant-poet' Robert Bloomfield, whom Constable liked to quote and who knew as much and more about real labour on the land, drew a similar line between life and art. His writings about rural life and landscape were called 'natural' and admired for portraying them before enclosure – a literary equivalent of Crome's *Mousehold Heath*. Constable would not have found common ground here. A Tory and an Anglican, he was more concerned about measures like the Reform Bill that threatened landed interests. Bloomfield's real similarity to Constable was that he too worked from recollection, having moved to London to work as a cobbler. He justified his poetic artistry with the hope that 'rural life by the art of cooking may be made a relishing and highly flavoured dish, whatever it may be in reality'.

I associate my 'careless boyhood' to all that lies on the banks of the *Stour*. They made me a painter (& I am gratefull)...
JOHN CONSTABLE

Constable's picture is a masterpiece
of retrospect as well as realism:
his father's death in 1816 dominated
its conception.

John Constable (1776–1837), *Flatford Mill ('Scene on a Navigable River')* 1816–17

OVERLEAF The Stour Valley

Peter de Wint (1784 – 1849), *Roman Canal, Lincolnshire* c.1840

Bloomfield died poor and forgotten save by a few fellow poets. The fate of John Clare, who wrote as the very poorest agricultural labourer in his *Poems Descriptive of Rural Life by a Northamptonshire Peasant* (1820), was worse: unhinged by an early move of a few miles across the Great Fen, madness removed him from his beloved countryside to an asylum in the town, and left him a living ghost. Failure or even martyrdom to landscape and rural life struck all of them and more in their lifetime. Clare admired Peter De Wint, painter of the huge fields and skies of Lincolnshire, for showing 'That misty flats, befringed with willow tree/Rivalled the beauties of the Italian skies', and begged a scrap of his work to hang on his cottage wall. But while De Wint had great success with his watercolours, he could find little market for his more rigorously detailed oils, which he hoarded in an attic gallery. Constable's pictures remained an acquired taste and although he was eventually honoured by the Royal Academy his vision seemed unlikely to live on. That it did was mainly due to his painter friend C.R. Leslie, whose *Memoirs of the Life of John Constable* (1843) pitted its hero, the painter of nature, against an unheeding domestic public and the cultural pretensions of Europe.

Leslie's book is a ringing assertion of Constable's Englishness. What it failed to do, despite offering a wealth of evidence and quoting the first use of the phrase 'Constable's Country', was to establish any prevailing sense of where the artist's art had been located. A cartoon in *Punch* in 1986, showing a couple in their car asking whether they have arrived at the 'right' Constable Country was not only about *types* of scenery, worthy of admiration or otherwise, but drew on a long and larger confusion, after it had been variously sited in the Midlands, Sussex and the West of England.

... a sad freak with which I have long been 'possessed' of feeling a duty – on my part – to tell the world that there is such a thing as landscape existing with 'Art' – as I have in so great a measure failed to 'show' the world that it is possible to accomplish it
JOHN CONSTABLE

By the end of the century however, Thomas Cook and the Great Eastern Railway were offering tours to the Stour valley, books on the area had appeared and local shops were stocking reproductions of Constable's pictures to enable an 'on site' comparison. Inasmuch as these places had ever looked exactly as he had painted them, they now did so less and less: Flatford Mill converted to steam power before closing altogether and Willy Lott's house disintegrated. This hardly mattered. Against a background of relative rural decline, Constable Country – which could be seen by extension to include much of the non-industrial South – became ever more precious as the epitome of yeoman England. To prove that all was not lost, that Britain's rural heart still beat, Flatford Mill and Lott's house were restored by the National Trust and are now leased to the Field Studies Council.

John Constable (1776–1837), *A Cornfield* ?1817

If Constable's Country did not exist, it would surely have been necessary to invent it. As work had grown scarce and conditions worse for the agricultural labourer, Joseph Arch's Revolt of the Fields of 1830 had spread from the Midlands to East Anglia. Farmer was set against farm-hand. Land went uncultivated and the villages emptied. What might be natural or true at such a time? Inspired by new technology, Peter Henry Emerson rejected subjective emotion to proclaim his naturalistic photography, then renounced naturalism for denying the artist's point of view. His photographs of East Anglians at work in field and fen resemble the French peasants painted by Jean-François Millet, whom he admired; they ignore progress to preserve the older world Emerson assumed was doomed. Today, in his own ongoing photographic survey 'The East Anglians', Justin Partyka shows us it was not. His stoical small farmers have survived two World Wars, economic slumps, mechanisation, urban 'overspill', nuclear power and the Bomb, hedge and woodland clearance, pesticides and crop-sprays. They exist at the margins of the present prosperity of European Union agricultural subsidies and colour-washed commuter land – itself perhaps a lull before new storms of brownfield development or loss of land to rising sea levels and global warming. Were they to speak, we might recognise the voices heard in Ronald Blythe's account of a composite Suffolk village, *Akenfield* (1969). Significantly, this marvellous book – which Peter Hall made into a film in 1974 – was not a collection of landscapes but of portraits, in which villagers, natives and newcomers, speak of themselves and their land.

Against such a background, evoking Constable's memory or landscape might seem more of a denial of reality than any he committed himself. David Murray's *In the Country of Constable* (1903) was an academic exercise, which followed Constable's footsteps safely back into the past. Patrick

> The clay acres themselves are the only tablet on which generations of village men have written, as John Clare did, *I am*.
> RONALD BLYTHE,
> Akenfield, 1969

Justin Partyka (born 1972), *Reed Cutting, Suffolk* 2004

Justin Partyka, *Sugar Beet Harvest, Norfolk* 2004

David Murray (1849–1933), *In the Country of Constable* 1903

George's *Hickbush* (1961–5) achieved a greater empathy by being painted in the open air on the artist's own patch of Suffolk at Grove Farm, to the same scale as Constable's larger works. It displays a slow, hard-won engagement with the agricultural landscape that he himself worked. By contrast, the East Anglian pastorals of Arnesby Brown are lyrical and escapist. His *Line of the Plough* (1919) shows the furrowed fields near Blakeney in Norfolk in harmony with the heavens, an antidote to the hell of the trenches. Brown painted wheeling birds. Forty years later, as Cedric Morris bitterly observed in his *Landscape of Shame* (*c.*1960), a protest

Patrick George (born 1923), *Hickbush* 1961–5

Arnesby Brown (1866–1955), *The Line of the Plough* exhibited 1919

against pesticides painted at his Suffolk home at Benton End, they were
more likely to fall dead. Peter Kennard, in a famous collage, predicted
greater horrors by loading Constable's *Hay Wain* with cruise missiles,
while Sydney Strube's cartoon, 'a long way after Constable' in the *Daily
Express* in 1929, bemoaned the new motoring economy by littering the
landscape with teashops (Willy Lott's house, no less), garages and advertise-
ments. Kennard's brilliant agitprop was adopted by the Campaign for
Nuclear Disarmament, and Strube's cartoon by the Council for the
Protection of Rural England for its 1929 exhibition, *Save the Countryside*.
Constable's quotation of an old villager crossing the Stour from Suffolk
to Essex – 'Goodbye Old England, I may never see you more' – now
seems prophetic, and the Flatford riverscape less a place of retreat than
a conduit for our fears and discontents.

Cedric Morris (1889–1982), *Landscape of Shame* c.1960

In the dampish green corner of Suffolk near Lord de Sausmarez's park, Shrublands, which William Coldstream painted in 1937, two men consult a map. Perhaps they have motored here, or come by train on the line that crosses the park. But having arrived, they look vulnerable and out of place. Inspired by W.H. Auden's fascination with maps as signifiers of progress, the artist called the picture *On the Map*, but the art historian Kenneth Clark, thinking they had lost their way, called it *Off the Map* when he lent

Peter Kennard (born 1949), *Hay Wain with Cruise Missiles* 1980

William Coldstream (1908–1987), *On the Map* 1937

it to Winston Churchill to hang in his wartime office. Curious indeed that such an ambiguous and disconcerting work should have been chosen to represent an English countryside worth fighting for; there are no easy answers here as to how it should be seen. Nor are they provided by Gilbert and George, in the monumental, composite charcoal-on-paper sculpture *The Nature of our Looking* (1970), which was made in London after the artists had been photographed by a friend walking in the fields near Colchester in the summer of 1970. With its play on the word 'nature', meaning both a way of doing something as well as the natural world itself, it asks how and what we see in such a landscape as this. On the Suffolk–Essex border, the art of Constable and Gainsborough is bound to spring to mind. The artists leave this to our imagination, but admit they may be pursuing a chimera; one section is inscribed: 'FOREVER WE WILL SEARCH AND GIVE OUR THOUGHTS TO THE PICTURE WE HAVE IN OUR MIND. WE ARE WALKING ROUND NOW AS SAD AS CAN BE.' This only makes more ironic the apparently respectful inscription on another section: 'HERE IN THE COUNTRY'S HEART WHERE THE GRASS IS GREEN, WE STAND VERY STILL AND QUIET.' This last comes partly from Norman Gale's poem 'The Country Faith' written, in a further irony, in 1914 as the villages were about to be decimated by the First World War:

HERE IN THE COUNTRY'S HEART   WHERE THE GRASS IS   GREEN WE STAND VERY   STILL AND QUIET

Gilbert and George (born 1943 and 1942), *The Nature of Our Looking* 1970 (detail)

Here in the country's heart
Where the grass is green,
Life is the same sweet life
As it e'er hath been

There is, of course, no such thing as an unchanging country, or country life. And that it had never been easy or idyllic is the message of another Suffolk poet, George Crabbe. He was a realist with a harder edge. For Byron, he was 'Nature's sternest painter, yet the best', and he himself set out to 'paint the cot/As Truth will paint it, and as Bards will not'.

Born in Aldeburgh, he was the author of *The Village* (1783), that unsmiling account of rural poverty in an infertile landscape, which, although written at Belvoir in Leicestershire, also contained his memories of coastal Suffolk. In *The Borough* (1810) he turned to the country town, really the coastal Aldeburgh itself. Its most famous character is the brutish Peter Grimes who grinds down his apprentices, then, in remorse, turns solitary and mad. This is a world of hearts as stony as the beaches with their surging tides, and as flinty as the towers of its churches. John Sell Cotman

John Sell Cotman (1782–1842), *Seashore with Boats c.*1808

Maggi Hambling (born 1945), tribute to Benjamin Britten, Aldeburgh, Suffolk

caught its bleakness in his views of the Norfolk shore. So too did the amateur Thomas Kerrich, vicar of Dersingham in north Norfolk, in his chalk sketches of vast skies and empty coast made in the 1790s. Turner's view of Aldeburgh, emphasising as it did a sunny post-Napoleonic mood, missed this special atmosphere. It comes, surely, from the power of the sea, which Benjamin Britten caught so well in the 'Sea Interludes' for his opera *Peter Grimes* (1945) – a power remorseless enough to sweep away the ancient port of Dunwich, and, perhaps, in years to come, the coasts and lands once reclaimed from it. Britten's chorus prays for deliverance from the tide. His own memorial, on Aldeburgh beach, bears Grimes's anguished cry: 'I hear those voices that will not be drowned.' Crabbe heard them too. For Wordsworth, 'Crabbe's Pictures are mere matters of fact; with which the Muses have just about as much to do as they have with a Collection of medical reports.' But the essayist William Hazlitt, ever perceptive, noted Crabbe's selective eye, his 'perverse and morbid taste' and focus on 'the most painful'; his poems are a 'funeral dirge over human life, but without pity, without hope'. On the coast as inland, an East Anglian claimed the truth and gave us art.

The Mystical West

Wales and the West Country have a curious feature in common. Their character runs in the opposite direction to their geography. Wales is divided between north and south, to the extent that it is often easier to travel between the two parts by going back into England. And although the map shows Devon and Cornwall as great slabs of the western peninsula of England, these counties divide naturally between north and south. The north has a rugged coastline while the south is relatively benign. The north is a hard place, the south softly curved, warmer, sunnier, and caressed by the Gulf Stream. The part I know best is the south, and particularly the South Devon coast. I came first as a teenager to the River Dart and have been back year after year to sail in my boat, *Rocket*, picnic on its shores and make forays to the little secret bays

"The journey begins at Stonehenge – the gateway to a magical kingdom of pre-historic ruins, ley lines, druids and bards, King Arthur and Merlin. As the road stretches westward across Salisbury Plain this curious circle of grey stones slips into view, if you are lucky with the setting sun behind it, or silhouetted against a stormy sky."

After J.M.W. Turner (1775–1851), *Stone Henge, Wiltshire* engraved by Robert Wallis 1829

Maiden Hill, Dorset

Eric Ravilious (1903–1942), *The Vale of the White Horse c.*1939

Llyn Padarn, Snowdon and Llanberis Pass

and beaches that can only be reached from the sea. It is a seductive coastline for the sailor. Unlike the east coast of Suffolk or Essex it has scenery looming above the water, great cliffs and steeply sloping hills. You can hear sheep calling to each other and in spring smell the scent of bluebells wafting off the slopes of Start Point. My favourite day is when the sun shines and the wind blows hard from the north west. It comes

across the land making for a flat sea in Start Bay and a chance to put a boat through its paces. There is even a measured mile marked on the beach to test *Rocket*'s speed.

The only drawback to this passion for the Dart is that it means I rarely venture far away. Once or twice I have cruised down the coast to Cornwall anchoring in friendly harbours like Salcombe and Fowey and ending in Falmouth and the

glorious Carrick Roads where *Rocket* was built. But the Mystical West has until now eluded me. Even the wilder rocky outcrops of Dartmoor and its rushing rivers have seemed too far to go, particularly in high summer when the traffic tails back along the narrow lanes that provide access to the moor. But from now on I shall look at the West and Wales in a new light.

I discovered in Scotland and the Lake District a curious passion for the landscape which was developed in the eighteenth and nineteenth century. In those days travellers seemed more determined to seek excitement from the natural phenomena that surrounded them. Today we go sailing, scuba diving, rock climbing and hang-gliding for our thrills. Back then it was the hills and mountains that provided a different kind of thrill, inducing terror and awe by their majesty. Sometimes this sensation can seem a little exaggerated, as though visitors were whipping themselves up into a frenzy of excitement, but on the whole it suggests a greater openness to the emotional impact of natural phenomena than we allow ourselves today. Nowhere is this more true than in the discovery of the Mystical West.

The journey begins at Stonehenge – the gateway to a magical kingdom of pre-historic ruins, ley lines, druids and bards, King Arthur and Merlin. As the road stretches westward across Salisbury Plain this curious circle of grey stones slips into view, if you are lucky with the setting sun behind it, or silhouetted against a stormy sky. It never fails to excite in its savagery. Stonehenge was at the centre of a growing interest in Britain's ancient past in the seventeenth and eighteenth centuries. Visitors experienced an 'ecstatic reverie' and gleefully speculated on the pagan rites that

might have been conducted around these stones.

It was at Stonehenge that John Constable and William Mallord Turner, those giants of English landscape painting, pitted their strengths against one another in a clash for mastery. Turner came first in 1811 and again in 1813 and made his first sketches. Constable arrived a few years later and enthused at a sight that carried him, as he put it, 'beyond all historical recall into the obscurity of a totally unknown period'. Some of his sketches, in my view still so much more accessible than his

Artists painting in the landscape, from the *Art Journal* (1887)

Laura Knight (1877–1970), *Spring* 1916–20

Lanyon Quoit, West Penwith

finished paintings, were drawn from identical viewpoints to those chosen by Turner. Turner upped the stakes with a dazzling painting of the ruins being struck by lightning. An engraving was made which sold well. But Constable came through as the victor with a painting which has been admired as the finest watercolour of his career from the day it was first exhibited at the Royal Academy in 1836. It is now in the Victoria and Albert Museum.

It would be wrong to think of landscape painting in the Mystical West without paying homage to

a native son of Wales – the great Richard Wilson who in the 1760s was painting in the wild landscape of Snowdonia and relishing untamed nature long before Constable and Turner or, for that matter, Wordsworth and Coleridge. Wilson relished the epic scale of the Welsh mountains most spectacularly perhaps in his famous painting of Cader Idris. His paintings in which humans appear to be dwarfed by the mountains around them can lay some claim to making Wales the true cradle of British landscape painting.

Go further west to St Ives on the

north coast of Cornwall and you come to a place which nurtured some of the best of twentieth century artists: Ben Nicholson, Christopher Wood, Peter Lanyon, Patrick Heron, Ivon Hitchens and Barbara Hepworth. It was here in the 1920s that the artistic community discovered the work of an unknown painter. Alfred Wallis was a retired fisherman who had taken up painting, untrained, on scraps of wood and cardboard. A painter whose work emerged from an ancient landscape untainted by the trappings of the art establishment, Wallis has given pleasure to millions by the simple beauty of his vision.

But it is not only painters who have been moved by the mystery of the West. In his novels Thomas Hardy used the name of the old kingdom for his home county of Dorset. The very word Wessex suggested something ancient and pagan. His characters in *Tess of the D'Urbervilles* or *The Return of the Native* seem to be ruled not by the morality of a Christian God but by their own passionate attachment to the landscape and the fate which waits for them there.

J.R.R. Tolkein came to Wales in 1904 when he was only twelve years old. He said later that he heard 'a call coming from the West'. It began with the names of railway stations as they flashed by, strange spellings and a language which 'pierced my

Graham Sutherland (1903–1980), *Black Landscape* 1939–40

linguistic heart'. He learnt Welsh and used it as the basis for the elvish language in *Lord of the Rings* and placed parts of Middle Earth in the mountains of mid-Wales.

And then there is Dylan Thomas who after years spent in London, like so many of his ambitious compatriots, returned to Wales for the final years of his life. His once prodigious poetic output had slowed, but the handful of poems he produced at that time are among his best, masterful and tender responses to the country around him. *Under Milk Wood*, which began life as *Quite Early One Morning*, remains to this day an icon of Wales and the Welsh.

The Mystical West is battling against encroaching civilisation which Hardy saw as the enemy. Villages grow into towns. Towns develop suburbs which rub noses with the next town. Roads are widened. Caravan sites and Visitor Centres proliferate in an attempt to keep the local economy alive now that coal and tin no longer provide a livelihood. But as long as painting and literature survive the old pagan world will keep its magic. You can see Cornwall as D.H. Lawrence did, as a window looking out of England. Or you can turn your back on the Atlantic and imagine you are looking in through a window towards Wales and and the West Country and see instead the rich variety of landscape stretching before you which has inspired some of our greatest painters and writers.

Myths and Megaliths

RICHARD HUMPHREYS

Alfred Watkins (1855–1935),
*Sacrificial Stone Aligning with
Giant's Cave Above It* 1924

OPPOSITE
Eric Ravilious (1903–1942), *The Vale
of the White Horse c.*1939 (detail)

FAIRY CHAINS

> She is not any common Earth
> Water or wood or air,
> But Merlin's Isle of Gramarye,
> Where you and I will fare
>
> Rudyard Kipling, quoted in
> Alfred Watkins, *The Old Straight Track*, 1925

Alfred Watkins was a late-Victorian Hereford businessman, who sold his brewery in 1898 to devote himself to his interests – photography, rowing, bee-keeping, debating, and local history. He took thousands of photographs of his native city and county, using his new exposure device the Bee Meter, which became a worldwide success. When he was younger he made his journeys by horse and gig; later in life he travelled in a variety of steam and then petrol-driven cars, eventually making his way through much of England and Wales. But his principal love remained the landscape of Herefordshire and the Welsh border country along Offa's Dyke, and he supplied the photographs for a local guide book in 1882 that recorded many man-made and natural features from oak trees and dovecots to megaliths and churchyard crosses.

However, Watkins is famous today as the man who conceived the idea of the 'ley line', or, as he titled his 1925 book, *The Old Straight Track* – a concept that he said came to him 'in a flash'. He recounted that in 1921, while on a visit to Blackwardine in Herefordshire, he saw, as in a vision, 'on the map a straight line starting from Croft Ambrey, lying on parts of Croft Lane past the Broad . . . over hill points, through Blackwardine, over Risbury Camp, and through the high ground at Stretton Grandison, where I surmise a Roman station'. He described it as a 'fairy chain' connecting natural and human sites such as hilltops and earthworks, and believed that this ancient network of tracks was created by primitive surveyors or 'dod men', and constituted the routes along which pre-historic man once travelled across Britain. He spent the last years of his life accumulating

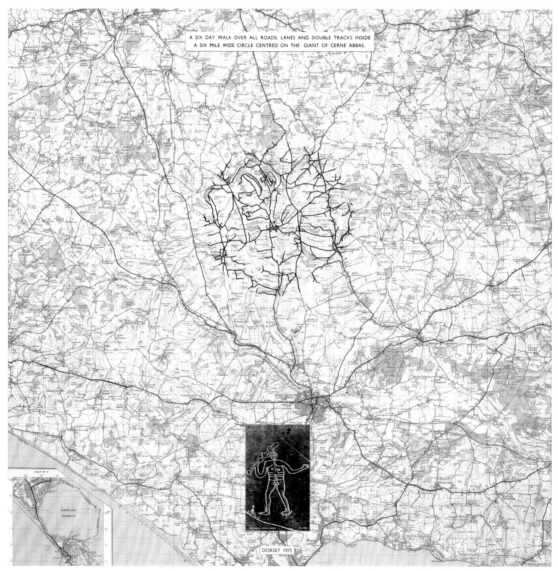

Richard Long (born 1945), *Cerne Abbas Walk* 1975

evidence for this theory, the genesis of which he ascribed to the many years of travelling that his 'other', unconscious, self had undertaken while his ordinary mind continued with its daily business. The books he wrote and the talks he gave on 'ley lines' (the term came from the number of significant place-names containing the syllable 'ley') led to the founding of ley-line clubs in the 1930s and, in the 1960s and 1970s, had an impact on the conceptual landscape work of such artists as Richard Long. It was also in the 1960s that ley lines were linked to flying-saucer flight paths, druids, crop circles and to fateful subterranean flows of earth energy, but these popular ideas took the concept far beyond Watkins's original controversial insight. Long's love of the ancient British landscape and of making works based on walks following certain geometrical forms can be seen in his *Cerne Abbas Walk* (1975). He walked along all roads and tracks within a six-mile-radius circle centred on the famous phallic giant at Cerne Abbas, leaving a trace in his work of a modern-day conceptual 'dod man'.

This mound in some remote and dateless day
Rear'd o'er a Chieftain of the Age of Hills
May here detain thee, Traveller! from thy road
Not idly lingering. In his narrow house
Some warrior sleeps below, whose gallant deeds
Haply at many a solemn festival
The Scauld hath sung; but perished is the song
Of praise, as o'er these bleak and barren downs
The wind that passes and is heard no more.
Go, traveller, and remember when the pomp
Of Earthly Glory fades, that one good deed,
Unseen, unheard, unnoted by mankind
Lives in the eternal register of heaven.

Robert Southey, Inscription for
a Plaque at Silbury Hill (1796)

Silbury Hill

YAWNING RUINS

The interest in 'ancient' Britain can be traced back many years before Alfred Watkins, however. It grew rapidly throughout the eighteenth century, building on the pioneering sixteenth- and seventeenth-century studies of history and folklore by scholars including William Camden, John Aubrey and John Evelyn, and was tied up with the nation's emerging sense of importance as an international power. Antiquarians and archaeologists, such as William Stukeley, excavated megalithic sites like Avebury in Wiltshire, drawing and recording their findings and speculating, often quite wildly, on their histories and meanings. These activities continue today among professional scholars, amateur enthusiasts and even latter-day druids, who are fascinated by the mysteries of sites from North Wales to Glastonbury and from Tintagel to Stonehenge. As British explorers and merchants came across Native Americans and other indigenous populations in their travels, they often recorded what they saw as parallels between these people and the early inhabitants of Britain.

In the 1630s the architect Inigo Jones had taken the view that Stonehenge could only have been built by the Romans, such was its sophistication and beauty. But a century later it was established that our so-called 'primitive' ancestors had created extraordinary civilisations and were entirely capable of building such structures. So great is their power that even today there are claims that aliens or Atlantans are the true makers of these amazing landscape forms, following earlier ideas that they were created by a lost race of giants or even by the devil.

From the sixteenth century onwards, artists made images of the barrows, stones and findings at these sites, which increasingly drew on highly imaginative ideas about the prehistoric peoples who had built them. These helped to create the image of Britain that a broadening audience was becoming aware of through illustrated books, prints and maps. Poets and other writers deepened the impact of this visual material by imagining ancient pasts and mythologising the distant roots of Europe's fastest-growing power. Debates about British ancestry and national identity saw a growing conviction that the British were an ancient people, and that the newly named 'United Kingdom', of which Scotland had become part in 1707, might find greater harmony through searching for a common past. For the English this past seemed

The great stones were then
in their wild state, so to speak.
Some were half-covered by the
grass, others stood up in cornfields
or were entangled and overgrown
in the copses, some were buried
under the turf. But they were
wonderful and disquieting, and as
I saw them then, I shall always
remember them.
PAUL NASH on Avebury c.1944

Avebury

Thomas Guest (1754–1818), *Grave Group from a Bell Barrow at Winterslow* 1814

to reside in the West, beginning near Stonehenge and extending to Wales and Cornwall.

In 1740 William Stukeley described the sensation of the 'yawning ruins' at Stonehenge as one of 'exstatic reverie, which none can describe, and they only can be sensible of it that feel it'. His drawings of Avebury and Stonehenge attempt to capture these 'sublime' feelings and he became increasingly fascinated by the signs of ancient life buried in the ground nearby. By 1814 we find the drawing master Thomas Guest painting four pictures of grave goods that had been excavated by the amateur archaeologist, the Revd A.B. Hutchins, from a Bronze Age bell barrow at Winterslow, a staging post on the turnpike road near Salisbury in Wiltshire. The one reproduced here shows an eight-inch-high beaker looming massively against the background of an uncultivated landscape that had been turned over to sheep grazing. The whole effect is dream-like, even surreal, with the new discoveries placed so as to create the maximum effect of surprise and a sense of disjunction between time and place, object and setting.

Over a century later Paul Nash painted *Equivalents for the Megaliths* (1935), coincidentally the year Guest's paintings were rediscovered. Nash was among a number of artists at this time who were deeply fascinated by British prehistoric culture and who saw it as offering great opportunities for the development of a distinctly national form of modern art. He had first visited Avebury in 1933 and had been inspired by the strange 'primal magic' of the megaliths there and by the surrounding Wiltshire landscape with its 'shaggy autumn grass':

These groups (at Avebury) are impressive as forms opposed to their surroundings both by virtue of their actual composition of lines and masses and planes, directions and volumes: and in the irrational sense, their suggestion of a super-reality. They are dramatic also, however, as symbols of their antiquity, as hallowed remains of an almost unknown civilisation.

Nash goes on to assert the over-riding importance for the modern artist of finding an aesthetic, rather than archaeological, response to the megaliths. He wanted to stress the mystery of the site by extracting a more abstract significance from it, rather than simply imitating its appearance. He was unhappy with the restoration of the stone-circle at Avebury in the 1930s by the millionaire archaeologist Alexander Keiller and felt the wilder presence he had encountered before Keiller's now familiar 'megalithic landscape gardening', to use the archaeologist Stuart Piggott's phrase, had been lost. Nash saw himself almost as a shaman-artist, able through a kind of formal magic to revitalise the mysterious ruins by making them utterly unfamiliar. Since the later nineteenth century the discipline of archaeology had established itself on a more scientific basis and artists were mainly employed as recorders of fact or, like Alan Sorrell, designers of plausible

Paul Nash (1889–1946), *Equivalents for the Megaliths* 1935

're-enactments' of by-gone times. Nash was asserting the artist's right to re-invent and imaginatively to rediscover ancient remains, rather than simply to record or theatrically animate them for educational purposes.

During the early nineteenth century it was artists such as John Constable and J.M.W. Turner who helped to make the great megalithic sites a part of the popular imagination and understanding of Britain's deep past. The philosopher Edmund Burke's idea of the 'sublime' as that which evokes feelings of danger and terror, obscurity and power, in art as well as in life, was by then familiar in artistic and literary circles. It provided the theoretical basis for a growing appreciation of desolate landscapes and ancient ruins. William Gilpin, the eighteenth-century theorist and populariser of the Picturesque, could find no pleasure in Stonehenge, yet within a generation it had become a site of particular fascination. As Burke wrote: 'Stonehenge, neither for disposition nor ornament, has anything admirable; but those huge rude masses of stone, set on end, and piled high on each other, turn the mind on the immense force necessary for such a work'. What seemed to many to be the bleak and barren Wiltshire landscape became wondrous on account of the apparently miraculous powers that brought Stonehenge into being. Wordsworth evoked this sense of wonder:

> Pile of Stone-henge! So proud to hint yet keep
> Thy secrets, thou lov'st to stand and hear
> The plain resounding to the whirlwind's sweep,
> Inmate of lonesome Nature's endless year.

Turner's striking print from his watercolour of 1828 uses lightning to suggest a landscape of biblical splendour and significance. He added stones that weren't there and rendered those that were incorrect in their dimensions. His aim was to evoke a place of terrifying supernatural

Edward McKnight Kauffer (1890–1954), *Stonehenge* 1931

Edward McKnight Kauffer's poster of Stonehenge was one of many Shell commissioned from artists between the two World Wars to encourage tourism by car owners.

William Overend Geller (1804–1881), *The Druid's Sacrifice* 1832

power. The print was enormously popular (see p.182) and the critic John Ruskin saw the original watercolour image as 'the standard of storm-drawing, both for the overwhelming power and gigantic proportions and spaces of its cloud forms, and for the tremendous qualities of lurid and sulphurous colours which are gained in them'.

Ruskin also regarded the lightning as a divine strike against pagan worship. This was a theme that became very popular in depictions of the great stones and survived well into the nineteenth century, until new historical research questioned the basis of Stukeley's influential belief in the druidical origins of the Stonehenge and Avebury circles. William Geller's lurid, best-selling mezzotint *The Druid's Sacrifice* of 1832 draws on the visual repertoire of the artist's mentor, the enormously popular painter of ancient sublimity, John Martin. A powerful burst of fiery light rising above Stonehenge illuminates a dark and stormy landscape populated by surging figures. This perhaps serves as another symbolic reminder of divine displeasure at the hideous rite of sacrifice that Geller shows being performed by 'idolatrous' priests.

One evening in June 1972, as I was preparing to sleep out for the night near Stonehenge, I saw another traveller arranging his sleeping bag beside a haystack. The following morning was the solstice. Some months later, after a conversation with Richard Long, I deduced he was the solitary figure I had seen, prior to his walk from Stonehenge to Glastonbury.

Hamish Fulton, from 'Old Muddy', *Richard Long: Walking in Circles*, 1991

Tintern Abbey and the Wye Valley

'A VERY INCHANTING PIECE OF SCENERY'

For many English tourists of the Romantic period, Stonehenge and Avebury were staging posts on the journey to Wales, a part of Britain that was becoming increasingly aware of its lost history and cultural heritage and re-establishing a strong sense of nationhood. In travelling there, tourists expected to find not only wonderful landscapes and buildings, but a whole way of life with a unique language and customs. The tourist route into Wales from the south and east was along the Wye Valley. Visitors travelled by boat from Ross-on-Wye in Herefordshire to Chepstow in South Wales, and thence into the bardic landscape popularised in poetry and guidebooks. The main attraction on the trip was a couple of hours at a Gothic ruin probably more agreeable to the general taste than mis-shapen megaliths. English travellers could visit Tintern Abbey and be reminded of their own lost Catholic past in this melancholy, beautiful spectacle of the ruined Cistercian abbey, which had been 'improved' and made more attractive for visitors in 1756 by the landowner, the Duke of Beaufort. William Gilpin made his celebrated journey up the Wye Valley in 1770, publishing his account of it in 1782.

For Gilpin this was the perfect Picturesque setting, except for what seemed to him to be some disappointing drawbacks: he found the building's remains 'ill-shaped' and suggested, remarkably, that 'a mallet judiciously used … might be of service in fracturing' some of the stones to give a more pleasing set of irregular shapes. He also warned of a nearby ironworks and some 'shabby houses', which could be avoided by adopting a suitable viewpoint.

> A more pleasing retreat could not easily be found. The woods, and glades intermixed; the winding of the river; the variety of the ground; the splendid ruin, contrasted with the objects of nature; and the elegant line formed by the summits of the hills, which include the whole; make all together a very inchanting piece of scenery.
>
> WILLIAM GILPIN

J.M.W. Turner (1775–1851), *The Chancel and Crossing of Tintern Abbey, Looking towards the East Window* 1794

North Wales was another favoured destination for English tourists and
artists in the late eighteenth century, and was usually approached via the
Wye Valley and Mid-Wales or from further north via Shropshire and
Cheshire. The artist who first established the region as a major focus of
artistic activity was the Welsh painter Richard Wilson, who was born at
Penegoes in mid-Wales, near Machynlleth, the capital of ancient Wales.
He had travelled extensively in Italy in the early 1750s and on his return
to London became the landscape painter of choice for an influential
group of aristocratic patrons. In Rome he had studied the art of the great
seventeenth-century French painters, Claude Lorrain and Nicholas Poussin,
and made his name initially as a painter of classical views of the city and
the surrounding *campagna*. In turning his attention to his native Welsh

Richard Wilson (1713–1782), *Snowdon from Llyn Nantlle* c.1765–6

In *Cader Idris*, literally 'the giant Idris's seat', Richard Wilson has exaggerated and reshaped much of the scenery in order to give it a greater presence. The small figures painting or looking through a Claude glass suggest a scene in which modern man exists in harmony with the natural world.

Richard Wilson (1713–1782), *Llyn-y-Cau, Cader Idris* exhibited ?1774

landscape from the later 1750s, Wilson used the pictorial devices he had developed in creating his Roman landscapes to invent a brilliant new 'Italian' vision of the Celtic landscape.

His view *Snowdon from Lyn Nantlle* demonstrates his approach, derived from Claude, of framing the view as if through a stage proscenium arch and creating a succession of planes leading from the peasant foreground figures to the distant summit of Snowdon (*Y Wydffa* in Welsh). The effect of Wilson's classicising style is to evoke a tranquil and ordered landscape, intended to appeal to the taste of his patron, in this case probably the major North Wales landowner William Vaughan. Significantly, Vaughan, a Welsh speaker, was first Chief President of the Honourable Society of the Cymmrodorion, a London-based group dedicated to the revival of ancient Welsh culture. It was indeed exiled Welsh nationalists, such as those who joined the Society of Cymmrodorion (a Welsh word meaning 'original inhabitants'), whose activities created the context in which Wilson's paintings of Wales were produced and admired. He appears to have been proud enough of Welsh scenery to consider it in no way inferior to any other landscape, and it is certainly the case that his other patrons, the writers George Lyttelton and Thomas Pennant, were equally enthusiastic about this hitherto largely unexplored world of mountains and waterfalls, ancient castles and lakes.

Wilson's *Llyn-y-cau, Cader Idris* was also bought by Vaughan and shows the view from the slopes of Mynydd Moel, one of the peaks on the Cader Idris ridge, down towards the volcanic lake near the summit of the mountain with the Bay of Cardigan in the distance. Wilson has exaggerated and reshaped much of the scenery in order to give it a greater presence, while the figures painting or looking through a glass suggest a scene in which modern man exists in harmony with the natural world. Cader Idris, literally 'the giant Idris's seat', was a site full of mythological meaning for nationalists. Some claimed it was the heart of King Arthur's kingdom, others that a night on the summit would either drive one mad or transform one into a poet. The lake was said to be bottomless. The giant Idris Gawr was one of the 'happy astronomers' of Welsh myth who supposedly made his observations from the summit.

By the late-eighteenth century the Welsh landscape was associated in the minds of both the Welsh and English with the idea of 'liberty'. Traditionally, Welsh history had been recorded orally and passed on by the bards. The preponderance of images of the 'last' Welsh bard, made popular through Thomas Gray's poem of the same name of 1757, underlines this theme. The myth of Edward I's order to annihilate all the bards, so that Welsh history could no longer be transmitted, appealed to a wide range of intellectuals, who saw the King's order as the face of oppressive authority, trying to obliterate the highest expression of natural freedom. In 1774,

Thomas Jones (1742–1803), *The Bard* 1774

William Williams (1758–1797), *Thunderstorm with the Death of Amelia* 1784

with the North Wales tourist business beginning to thrive, Wilson's pupil, Thomas Jones, painted the last, tragic bard about to hurl himself into the River Conwy. Stonehenge, which Jones had visited a few years earlier and admired for its druidical atmosphere, has been transported to the middle distance with Snowdon and an advancing English army visible on the horizon.

Despite its growing popularity with tourists, Wales was perceived as one of as the dangerous wildlands of Britain in the late eighteenth-century imagination. Jones was not alone in turning to the stormier style of the Italian seventeenth-century artist Salvator Rosa to achieve his melo-dramatic effects. The itinerant theatrical painter William Williams's *Thunderstorm with the Death of Amelia* (1784) takes its subject from 'Summer' in James Thomson's poetic cycle *The Seasons*. Published in 1730, and probably the most important landscape poem of the eighteenth century, Williams depicts the tragic conclusion to a lovers' stroll as the poem's heroine Amelia is struck by lightning and collapses into the hero Celadon's arms. He sets his sublime drama in Caernarvonshire, with Snowdon in the distance behind an ancient castle on a huge rocky outcrop. In the foreground, as if on a stage, an oak tree is split in two, like the love of the central characters, with its fantastical branches falling to the ground.

WILD WALES

By the mid-nineteenth century Wales was a popular destination for large numbers of tourists and artists, who were attracted by the landscape, the lifestyle and the atmosphere of what was now known as 'Wild Wales'. Samuel Palmer had painted visionary landscapes in Shoreham, Kent during the 1820s, and was the leading member of the circle that called themselves 'The Ancients', but by the 1830s he was looking for new subjects. In 1835 and 1836 he travelled to Wales in the company of fellow artist Edward Calvert in search of what he called 'Ossian Sublimities'. His remarkable study of the light, water and spray at the falls at Pistil Mawddach, north of Dolgellau, shows a move to a naturalism in art that found beauty in the scientific observation of the landscape.

Further north, where the Lugwy and Lledr rivers meet the Conwy, lies Betws-y-coed, a small village that became an artists' colony in the 1850s after the Birmingham painter David Cox began to spend long summers there from 1844. Cox had visited Wales since 1805 and in 1836 illustrated Thomas Roscoe's popular book *Wanderings and Excursions in North Wales*.

Swallow Falls, Betws-y-Coed

Samuel Palmer (1805–1881), *The Waterfalls, Pistil Mawddach, North Wales* 1835–6

The local population spoke Welsh, dressed 'picturesquely' and seemed to lead the idyllic life of which urban artists and tourists dreamed. While local beauty spots such as the 'Fairy Glen' were a main attraction, it was the 'Celtic' way of life that was so alluring for the growing numbers of visitors drawn to the alleged site of Edward I's 'Massacre of the Bards'.

In about 1847 Cox, a devout Nonconformist, witnessed the evening funeral ceremony of a young girl and made a number of studies of it, leading to a popular print of 1862. In its depiction of a traditional rural funeral his painting is reminiscent of the French painter Gustave Courbet's celebrated *Burial at Ornans* (1850). It shows a pious and humble community unified under the protective Welsh landscape that determines their fate. Ironically, Cox's famous image was to contribute to the huge increase in building at Betws-y-Coed, which was a result of the village's popularity among 'BTs', as the British tourists were dubbed by the painter Thomas Collier.

By the early twentieth century many Welsh painters shared the cultural aims of the nationalist movement, expressed in festivals such as the famous Eisteddfod, and were among those who processed to Richard Wilson's grave in Mold, North Wales, to lay a wreath there in 1923. The continuing fascination with ancient myth can be seen in the work of the Manchester-born painter Henry Clarence Whaite. He had been influenced by Cox's art

David Cox (1783–1859), *A Welsh Funeral, Betws–y–Coed* c.1847–50

Henry Clarence Whaite (1828–1912), *Arthur in the Gruesome Glen* c.1908

and personality, and by John Ruskin's ideas about faith and natural study, and spent most of his career painting the landscape and life of a country where he eventually settled in 1870. His work sometimes inclined towards a kind of Protestant mysticism, more potent than the gentle moral atmosphere of Cox's *Welsh Funeral*. His huge *Arthur in the Gruesome Glen* is an epic Edwardian return to the dramatic sublimity of Jones and Williams before him. He had been a leading figure in the new Royal Cambrian Academy of Art from its foundation in 1882, and this work is no doubt an 'academic machine' inspired by the grandiose themes of Turner and more recently the work of the symbolist painter George Frederick Watts.

The early twentieth century also saw new developments in art, rendering both Whaite's grand romance and the Pre-Raphaelite approach to landscape out-of-date to many. When the Welsh-born artists Augustus John and James Dickson Innes first travelled together to Wales in 1911, they did so in full knowledge of Post-Impressionism and other new styles that had emerged from Paris over the previous twenty years, led by artists such as Paul Gauguin and Henri Matisse. In search of a new art, they painted luminous landscapes of mountains and lakes that were unlike anything previously

James Dickson Innes (1887–1914), *Arenig, North Wales* 1913

In the catalogue of the 1923 memorial exhibition of James Dickson Innes's work, Augustus John stated that the artist had made the mountain of Arenig 'his own', as Cézanne had done with Mont Sainte Victoire in Provence.

produced in Wales. Over the course of the next few years, based at a cottage at Nant-Ddu in North Wales, John and Innes painted the same views together in often strikingly similar fashion. John was convinced of Innes's innate *naïveté*, a quality that he valued above all, often proclaiming 'Let us be as children!' Innes, who died of tuberculosis at the age of twenty-seven, was a romantic, youthful figure and in John's view a natural 'child of the valleys' – the painterly counterpart to the literary bards of Welsh tradition. In the catalogue of the 1923 memorial exhibition of Innes's work, John stated that the artist had made the mountain of Arenig 'his own', as Cézanne had done with Mont Sainte Victoire in Provence. The bright blues and pinks of his paintings of Arenig, seen over Lake Bala, and the simple lines of the drawing, seemed to John the epitome of the work of a brilliant and uninhibited child-like artist.

NEW ROMANTICS

South Wales came into its own as a site for artistic interpretation during the 1940s. The English painter Graham Sutherland had visited Pembrokeshire regularly in the 1930s and created a modernist vision of the landscape that nevertheless accentuated a strong sense of place and of 'Celtic' mystery. His *Black Landscape* (1939–40, p.187) depicts a view looking north-west from the village of Porth Clais (near the cathedral city of St David's), towards the rocky outcrop of Clegyr-Boia. There is an ominous brooding quality to the work, painted when Sutherland was evacuated from his Kent home during the Christmas of 1939, and the black and pink tonality seem to bring the threat of war to the remote south western area of Wales to which he and his wife had withdrawn. Sutherland was deeply influenced by Palmer's Shoreham images and also by Palmer's mentor, William Blake. Like Blake and Palmer, he believed in what he called 'intrinsic' drawing that submerges externally viewed material 'in the reservoir of the subconscious mind out of which emerge the reconstructed and re-created images'.

Sutherland, who was an official war artist in the industrial towns of Wales, was followed west during the war by a number of younger artists who have since become known as 'Neo-Romantics'. Characterised by the emphasis in their paintings on the inner and symbolic meanings of the landscape, they included David Jones, Ceri Richards, John Piper and John Minton. While Jones developed a 'Celtic' art to complement his dense literary work, Minton responded more physically to the landscape. His ink drawing *Recollections of Wales* (1944) is set in north Wales. A masculine female figure stands under a tree on the left and looks out across a tortuously elaborate landscape, which seems to flow from her head and hair. The tension of the relationship between figure and setting is acute – a nostalgic sense of loss and longing is charged with an intense and ambiguous sexuality. Here is a compromised and threatened innocence, an endangered pastoral far from the Mediterranean ease and simplicity of Innes's vision before the First World War.

John Minton (1917–1957), *Recollections of Wales* 1944

'DESCRIBING THE INVISIBLE': THE ART OF ST IVES

Following the Second World War the fishing village of St Ives on the West
Penwith peninsula of Cornwall became a major destination for artists,
much as nearby Newlyn had been at the end of the nineteenth century.
Its distinctly Celtic landscape, language and culture gave it the same exotic
allure as Wales. The painters Ben Nicholson and Christopher Wood first
discovered inspiration in St Ives in 1928, Wood finding there a similarity
with the fishing ports of Brittany that he had recently been painting. Most
importantly, they had by chance encountered an old, illiterate fisherman,
Alfred Wallis, who in his lonely, widowed retirement had turned to
painting. Applying house paint to a range of surfaces from walls to pieces
of cardboard, Wallis, who was entirely self-taught, painted his experiences
as a fisherman from memory. He also painted St Ives itself, composing
his views so that they fitted the odd shapes of the surfaces on which he
worked. Referring to Wallis, Nicholson wrote in 1943: 'Using the materials

Alfred Wallis (1855–1942), 'The Hold House Port Mear Square Island
Port Mear Beach' c.1932

Alfred Wallis with Ben Nicholson

Ben Nicholson (1894–1982), *1943–45 (St Ives, Cornwall)* 1943–5

to hand is the motive and method of the first artist. Certainly his vision is a remarkable thing, with an intensity and depth of experience which makes it more than childlike.' Again we see the value placed on a primitive and childlike quality, with Wallis regarded by his fellow artists as a kind of pictorial bard, drawing from his inner nature and making use of the simple materials around him. Nicholson's ideas are taken from a number of writers who saw art as a channel for a renewed and innocent vision of the world. What better protagonist for those who held such views than an uneducated old sea man, full of memories, making art from his life and from the things available nearby?

Nicholson's wife, the sculptor Barbara Hepworth, had moved with him to St Ives at the start of the war. Her painted wooden sculpture *Pelagos* of 1946 captures the strange mixture of Mediterranean and Atlantic fantasy typical of St Ives art, as well as drawing on the complex response to landscape of Sutherland and the Neo-Romantic artists. Hollowed out from an ovoid ball of polished elm, *Pelagos* is painted matt blue inside. The two curving arms formed by the carving are joined by taut strings, creating the impression of an ancient musical instrument. The title of the piece comes from the Greek word for 'sea' and Hepworth later explained some of the meaning of the work, which was inspired by the view from her studio over Carbis Bay:

> I could see the whole bay of St Ives, and my response to this view was that of a primitive who observes the curves of a coast and horizon and experiences, as he faces the ocean, a sense of containment and security rather than the dangers of an endless expanse of waters. So *Pelagos* represents not so much what I saw as what I felt.

Hepworth, notably invoking the mind of 'primitive man' faced by the horror of the 'sublime' spoke of 'becoming the object' in making such sculptures. Their painted interiors 'plunged me into the depth of water, caves or shadows deeper than the carved concavities themselves . . . the strings were the tensions I felt between myself and the sea, the wind or the hills'. These expressions are derived from the language of psychoanalysis and are typical of the ideas through which such semi-abstract art came into being in the 1930s and 1940s in Britain. Like her St Ives friend, the painter, critic and psychoanalytical theorist Adrian Stokes, Hepworth saw art as a means, through a deep response to landscape, to integrate the inner

Barbara Hepworth (1903–1975), *Pelagos* 1946

and outer worlds during a century of damaging psychic and political division.

Peter Lanyon was born in West Penwith, and was also a modernist painter who trained with Nicholson. A bardic figure who was no longer isolated from the broader currents of European culture, nor from modernity in general, he seemed to be almost the spiritual progeny of Wallis and his teacher. He was engaged with the history, meanings and physicality of his native landscape and, like Hepworth and Sutherland, searched for a balance between the inner and outer worlds through an art that combined abstraction and representation. He was also keenly interested in new technologies, however, and in particular those of flight. Lanyon began gliding in 1959 and his work soon reflected this new experience and his identification with the natural world of wind and bird flight. He wrote of his work *Thermal* (1960) that as well as evoking glider flight it was:

> concerned with birds describing the invisible, their flight across cliff faces and their soaring activity. The air is a very definite world of activity as complex and demanding as the sea . . . The thermal itself is a current of hot air rising and eventually condensing into cloud. It is invisible and can only be apprehended by an instrument such as a glider . . . The picture refers to cloud formation and to a spiral rising activity which is the way a glider rises in an up-current.

Peter Lanyon (1918–1964), *Thermal* 1960

Lanyon was killed in a gliding accident in 1964, a tragedy memorialised by the St Ives poet W.S. Graham in his poem 'The Thermal Stair'. Graham writes of the painter steering his life 'to maim himself somehow for the job'. His final lines seem to evoke the lasting power of the fated Romantic, bardic artist we have found throughout the Mystical West:

> Uneasy, lovable man, give me your painting
> Hand to steady me taking the word-road home.
> Lanyon, why is it you're earlier away?
> Remember me wherever you listen from.
> Lanyon, dingdong dingdong from carn to carn.
> It seems tonight all closing bells are tolling
> Across the Duchy shire wherever I turn.

LIST OF ILLUSTRATED WORKS

Within each section works are listed alphabetically by artist, with page references in brackets. Dimensions are given in millimetres, height before width. The owners of the works have provided photographs unless otherwise indicated.

INTRODUCTION

Claude Lorrain (1600–1682)
Landscape with Hagar and the Angel 1646 (p.11)
Oil on canvas mounted on wood
522 × 423
The National Gallery, London

Edwin Smith (1912–1971)
Gordale Scar, Yorkshire 1969 (p.20)
Gelatin-silver print 252 × 202
Victoria and Albert Museum, London

Graham Sutherland (1903–1980)
Green Tree Form: Interior of Woods 1940 (p.15)
Oil on canvas 787 × 1079
Tate. Purchased 1940

THE ROMANTIC NORTH

Conrad Atkinson (born 1940)
For Wordsworth; for West Cumbria 1980 (p.48)
Photograph, acrylic and mixed media on board
52.1 × 62.2
Tate. Purchased 1981

Dora Carrington (1893–1932)
Farm at Watendlath 1921 (p.47)
Oil on canvas 611 × 669
Tate. Presented by Noel Carrington, the artist's brother 1987

Julian Cooper (born 1949)
Large Honister Crag 2003–2004 (p.30)
Oil on canvas 2140 × 1530
Tullie House Museum and Art Gallery

John Crome (1768–1821)
Slate Quarries circa 1802–5 (p.34)
Oil on canvas 1238 × 1587
Tate. Purchased 1878

James Durden (1878–1964)
Summer in Cumberland 1925 (p.53)
Oil on canvas 1015 × 1015
Manchester City Galleries

Thomas Girtin (1775–1802)
Bamburgh Castle, Northumberland c.1797–9 (p.23)
Watercolour, gouache and pencil on paper
549 × 451
Tate. Presented by A.E. Anderson in memory of his brother Frank through the National Art Collections Fund 1928

Atkinson Grimshaw (1836–1893)
Bowder Stone, Borrowdale c.1863–8 (pp.28, 31)
Oil on canvas 400 × 536
Tate. Purchased with assistance from the Friends of the Tate Gallery 1983

Benjamin Robert Haydon (1786–1846)
William Wordsworth 1842 (p.43)
Oil on canvas 1245 × 991
National Portrait Gallery, London

Thomas Hearne (1744–1817)
Sir George Beaumont and Joseph Farington Sketching a Waterfall c.1777 (pp.19, 32)
Watercolour wash over pen and ink on paper
445 × 292
The Wordsworth Trust, Grasmere

Benjamin Williams Leader (1831–1923)
The Excavation of the Manchester Ship Canal: Eastham Cutting, with Mount Manisty in the Distance 1891 (p.52)
Oil on canvas 1245 × 2120
The National Trust (Tatton Park, Cheshire)
Photo: John Hammond

L.S. Lowry (1887–1976)
Industrial Landscape 1955 (p.51)
Oil on canvas 1143 × 1524
Tate. Presented by the Trustees of the Chantrey Bequest 1956

Stanley Royle (1888–1961)
Sheffield from Wincobank Wood 1923 (p.29)
Oil on canvas 711 × 918
Sheffield Galleries & Museums Trust
Photo: www.bridgeman.co.uk

Francis Towne (1739–1816)
Waterfall near Ambleside 1786 (p.33)
Pen and ink and watercolour on paper
380 × 265
Tate. Purchased as part of the Oppé Collection with assistance from the National Lottery through theHeritage Lottery Fund 1996

J.M.W. Turner (1775–1851)
Morning amongst the Coniston Fells, Cumberland exh.1798 (p.38)
Oil on canvas 1229 × 899
Tate. Bequeathed by the artist 1856

Shields, on the River Tyne 1823 (p.50)
Watercolour on paper 154 × 216
Tate. Bequeathed by the artist 1856

Norham Castle, Sunrise 1798 (p.39)
Pencil, watercolour and bodycolour on paper
501 × 705
Trustees of the Cecil Higgins Art Gallery, Bedford

James Ward (1769–1859)
Gordale Scar (A View of Gordale, in the Manor of East Malham in Craven, Yorkshire, the Property of Lord Ribblesdale) ?1812–14, exh. 1815 (p.35)
Oil on canvas 3327 × 4216
Tate. Purchased 1878

THE HOME FRONT

John Constable (1776–1837)
Chain Pier, Brighton 1826–7 (p.68)
Oil on canvas 1270 × 1829
Tate. Purchased 1950

William Dyce (1806–1864)
Pegwell Bay, Kent – a Recollection of October 5th 1858 ?1858–60 (p.69)
Oil on canvas 635 × 889
Tate. Purchased 1894

William Powell Frith (1819–1909)
The Derby Day 1856–8 (p.64)
Oil on canvas 1016 × 2235
Tate. Bequeathed by Jacob Bell 1859

H.G. Gawthorn (1879–1941)
Women's Land Army (God Speed the Plough and the Woman who Drives It) c.1917 (p.73)
Poster
Imperial War Museum, London

James Gillray (1757–1815)
The French Invasion; – or – John Bull, bombarding the Bum-Boats (p.63)
Hand-coloured etching 350 × 250
The British Museum, London

William Holman Hunt (1827–1910)
Our English Coasts, 1852 ('Strayed Sheep') 1852 (p.72)
Oil on canvas 432 × 584
Tate. Presented by the National Art Collections Fund 1946

John Linnell (1792–1882)
Harvest Moon 1858 (p.71)
Oil on wood 378 × 460
Tate. Bequeathed by Mrs E.J. Thwaites 1955

Thomas Monnington (1902–1976)
Southern England, Tempests attacking Flying–Bombs 1944 (p.80)
Oil on canvas 901 × 1143
Imperial War Museum, London

Henry Moore (1898–1986)
Tube Shelter Perspective 1941 (p.79)
Pencil, ink, wax and watercolour on paper, unique 483 × 438
Tate. Presented by the War Artists Advisory Committee 1946

Frank Newbould (1887–1951)
Your Britain, Fight for it Now (Salisbury Cathedral) 1942 (p.78)
Poster
Imperial War Museum, London

Your Britain, Fight for it Now (The South Downs) 1942 (p.58–9, 78)
Poster
Imperial War Museum, London

John Nash (1893–1977)
The Cornfield 1918 (p.76)
Oil on canvas 686 × 762
Tate. Presented by the Contemporary Art Society 1952

Paul Nash (1889–1946)
The Battle of Britain 1941 (pp.60, 83)
Oil on canvas 1240 × 1840
Imperial War Museum, London

Totes Meer (Dead Sea) 1940–1 (p.82)
Oil on canvas 1016 × 1524
Tate. Presented by the War Artists Advisory Committee 1946

Samuel Palmer (1805–1881)
Coming from Evening Church 1830 (p.71)
Mixed media on gesso on paper 302 × 200
Tate. Purchased 1922

Philip Wilson Steer (1860–1942)
The Beach at Walberswick ?c.1889 (p.70)
Oil on wood 603 × 761 × 15
Tate. Purchased 1942

A Procession of Yachts 1892–3 (p.65)
Oil on canvas 629 × 762
Tate. Purchased 1922

Henry Scott Tuke (1858–1929)
August Blue 1893–4 (p.70)
Oil on canvas 1219 × 1829
Tate. Presented by the Trustees of the Chantrey Bequest 1894

J.M.W. Turner (1775–1851)
The Shipwreck 1805 (p.62)
Oil on canvas 1705 × 2416
Bequeathed by the artist 1856

HIGHLANDS AND GLENS

Michael Andrews (1928–1995)
Alistair's Day: 2nd Stalk 1980 (p.112)
Acrylic on canvas 1830 × 1830
Private collection

David Young Cameron (1865–1945)
Wilds of Assynt c.1936 (pp.90, 114)
Oil on canvas 1021 × 1279
Perth Museum & Art Gallery
Photo: P. Adair

George Cruikshank (1792–1878)
Geordie and Willie "keeping it up" – Johnny Bull Pays the Piper 1822 (p.110)
Etching on paper 116 × 193
The British Museum, London

Thomas Faed (1826–1900)
The Last of the Clan 1865 (p.94)
Oil on canvas 863 × 1117
Fleming Collection, London
Photo: The Fleming-Wyfold Art Foundation/ www.bridgeman.co.uk

Hamish Fulton (born 1946)
Seven Days Walking and Seven Nights Camping in a Wood, Scotland, March 1985 1985
Photo: Courtesy of the Artist

Paul Henry (1876–1958)
On Killary Bay, Connemara c.1930–9 (p.88)
Oil on board 355 × 405
Photo: www.Bridgeman.co.uk

David Octavius Hill (1802–1870)
A View of Edinburgh from North of the Castle 1859 (p.98)
Oil on panel 810 × 1550
Royal Bank of Scotland, Edinburgh

John Knox (1778–1845)
Landscape with Tourists at Loch Katrine c.1820 (pp.8, 108)
Oil on canvas 900 × 1250
The National Gallery of Scotland

Edwin Henry Landseer (1802–1873)
Monarch of the Glen (p.93)
Oil on canvas 1994 × 2056
Lent by Diageo Ltd

Horatio McCulloch (1805–1867)
My Heart's in the Highlands 1860 (p.92)
Oil on canvas 610 × 914
Glasgow Museums: Art Gallery & Museum, Kelvingrove

William McTaggart (1835–1910)
The Emigrants 1883–9 (p.100)
Oil on canvas 946 × 1410
Tate. Purchased 1931

Alexander Nasmyth (1758–1840)
Castle Huntly, Perthshire c.1810 (p.99)
Oil on canvas 1149 × 1708
McManus Galleries, Dundee Museums & Art Galleries

218

Henry Raeburn (1756–1823)
Francis MacNab, "The MacNab" exh. 1819 (p.96)
Oil on canvas 2413 × 1524
Diageo Ltd

Thomas Miles Richardson (1813–1890)
Glencoe 1853 (p.106)
Watercolour on paper 300 × 500
Fleming Collection, London
Photo: www.bridgeman.co.uk

Gourlay Steell (1819–1894)
A Highland Parting 1885 (p.111)
Oil on canvas 1321 × 1753
McManus Galleries, Dundee Museums &
Art Galleries

Edward Arthur Walton (1860–1922)
Berwickshire Field-Workers 1884 (p.115)
Oil on canvas 914 × 609
Tate. Purchased 1982

Jack Butler Yeats (1871–1957)
Morning After Rain 1923 (p.87)
Oil on canvas 610 × 914
Tate. Presented by the Friends of the
Tate Gallery 1964

THE HEART OF ENGLAND

James Bateman (1893–1959)
Haytime in the Cotswolds 1939 (p.149)
Oil on canvas 1068 × 1338
Southampton City Art Gallery
Photo: www.bridgeman.co.uk

Edwin Butler Bayliss (1874–1950)
Evening in the Black Country c.1910 (p.141)
Oil on canvas 500 × 600
Wolverhampton Art Museums

Bernd Becher and Hilla Becher (born 1931, 1934)
Pitheads 1974 (p.120)
Photograph on board 1133 × 1318
Tate. Purchased 1974

J.C. Bourne (1773–1854)
*Drawings of the London and Birmingham
Railway* 1839 (p.140)
Engraving on paper
National Railway Museum
Photo: Science & Society Picture Library

David Cox (1783–1859)
The Night Train c.1849 (p.139)
Watercolour on paper 276 × 373
Birmingham Museums & Art Gallery

Philip James de Loutherbourg (1740–1812)
Coalbrookdale by Night 1801 (p.133)
Oil on canvas 680 × 1067
Science Museum, London
Photo: Science & Society Picture Library

Dickinson Brothers
Waiting for the Queen 1851 (p.140)
Lithograph on paper
Ironbridge Gorge Museum Trust, Elton collection

F.L. Griggs (1876–1938)
Duntisbourne Rouse 1927 (p.146)
Watercolour on paper
Ashmolean Museum, Oxford

Samuel Hieronymous Grimm (1733–1794)
Cresswell Crags, Derbyshire 1785 (p.127)
Watercolour and pen and ink on paper 259 × 372
Tate. Purchased as part of the Oppé Collection
with assistance from the National Lottery
through the Heritage Lottery Fund 1996

John Rogers Herbert (1810–1890)
Laborare est Orare 1862 (p.142)
Oil on canvas 972 × 1759
Tate. Purchased 1971

Alfred Powell (1865–1960)
Punch Bowl with views of Gloucestershire 1928
(p.148)
Earthenware, painted in underglaze blue
310 × 380 × 380
Cheltenham Art Gallery & Museum
Photo: www.bridgeman.co.uk

John Rose & Co.
*Mug with a view of Iron Bridge and
Buildwas Abbey* (p.134)
Ceramic mug
Ironbridge Gorge Museum Trust

William Rothenstein (1872–1945)
Barn at Cherington, Gloucestershire 1935 (p.147)
Oil on canvas
610 × 749
Tate. Bequeathed by the artist 1946

John Singer Sargent (1856–1925)
Lady Fishing – Mrs Ormond 1889 (p.145)
Oil on canvas 1848 × 978
Tate. Presented by Miss Emily Sargent in
memory of her brother through the National
Art Collections Fund 1929

George Stubbs (1724–1806)
Horse Frightened by a Lion ?exhibited 1763 (p.126)
Oil on canvas 705 × 1019
Tate. Purchased with assistance from
the National Heritage Memorial Fund,
the National Art Collections Fund and the
Friends of the Tate Gallery 1994

Edward Wadsworth (1889–1949)
Black Country 1919 (p.120)
Woodcut on paper 110 × 145
Victoria & Albert Museum

William Williams (1758–1797)
View of Ironbridge 1780 (p.135)
Oil on canvas 745 × 893
Ironbridge Gorge Museum Trust

Joseph Wright (1734–1797)
Arkwright's Cotton Mills by Night c.1782–1783
(p.131)
Oil on canvas 997 × 1257
Private collection
Photo: www.bridgeman.co.uk

Sir Brooke Boothby 1781 (p.130)
Oil on canvas 1486 × 2076
Tate. Bequeathed by Miss Agnes Ann Best 1925

An Iron Forge Viewed from Without 1773 (pp.124, 132)
Oil on canvas 1213 × 1320
State Hermitage Museum, St Petersburg

Matlock Tor by Daylight mid–1780s (p.129)
Oil on canvas 635 × 762
Fitzwilliam Museum, Cambridge

THE FLATLANDS

Richard Billingham (born 1970)
Untitled, Norfolk (Dyke) 2003 (p.159)
Lightjet colour print on paper 1260 × 1545
The Artist, c/o Anthony Reynolds Gallery

Untitled Norfolk (Cows) 2003 (p.158)
Lightjet colour print on paper 830 × 1030
The Artist, c/o Anthony Reynolds Gallery

Arnesby Brown (1866–1955)
The Line of the Plough exhibited 1919 (p.176)
Oil on canvas 635 × 762
Tate. Presented by the Trustees of the
Chantrey Bequest 1919

William Coldstream (1908–1987)
On the Map 1937 (p.178)
Oil on canvas 508 × 508
Tate. Purchased 1980

John Constable (1776–1837)
Flatford Mill ('Scene on a Navigable River')
1816–17 (pp.156, 169)
Oil on canvas 1016 × 1270
Tate. Bequeathed by Miss Isabel Constable as the
gift of Maria Louisa, Isabel and Lionel Bicknell
Constable 1888

The Mill Stream c.1810 (p.167)
Oil on board 210 × 292
Tate. Bequeathed by Henry Vaughan 1900

A Cornfield ?1817 (p.173)
Oil on canvas 613 × 510
Tate. Accepted by HM Government in lieu of
Inheritance Tax and allocated to Tate 2004

John Sell Cotman (1782–1842)
Seashore with Boats c.1808 (p.180)
Oil on board 283 × 410
Tate. Purchased 1935

John Crome (1768–1821)
Moonrise on the Yare c.1811–16 (p.154)
Oil on canvas 711 × 1111
Tate. Bequeathed by George Salting 1910

Mousehold Heath, Norwich c.1818–20 (p.164)
Oil on canvas 1099 × 1810
Tate. Purchased 1863

The Poringland Oak c.1818–20 (p.163)
Oil on canvas 1251 × 1003
Tate. Purchased 1910

The Steam Packet 1813–17 (p.165)
Oil on canvas 515 × 424
Manchester City Galleries

Peter de Wint (1784–1849)
Roman Canal, Lincolnshire c.1840 (p.172)
Watercolour on paper 238 × 549
Tate. Bequeathed by John Henderson 1879

Thomas Gainsborough (1727–1788)
'Gainsborough's Forest' (Cornard Wood) c.1748 (p.161)
Oil on canvas 1219 × 1549
The National Gallery, London

Gilbert and George (born 1943, born 1942)
The Nature of Our Looking 1970 (p.179)
Hand-coloured drawing on paper
Tate. Purchased 1982

Patrick George (born 1923)
Hickbush 1961–5 (p.175)
Oil on canvas 1060 × 1524
Tate. Presented by the Trustees of the
Chantrey Bequest 1967

Thomas Hearne (1744–1817)
View in Suffolk 1776 (p.162)
Watercolour on paper 357 × 522
Leeds City Art Gallery
Photo: www.bridgeman.co.uk

Peter Kennard (born 1949)
Haywain with Cruise Missiles 1980 (p.177)
Photo montage
Collection of the artist

Cedric Morris (1889–1982)
Landscape of Shame c.1960 (p.177)
Oil on canvas 756 × 1002
Tate. Presented by the Friends of
the Tate Gallery 1987

David Murray (1849–1933)
In the Country of Constable 1903 (p.175)
Oil on canvas 1219 × 1829
Tate. Presented by the Trustees of the
Chantrey Bequest 1903

Justin Partyka (born 1972)
Reed Cutting, Suffolk 2004 (p.174)
Sugar Beet Harvest, Norfolk 2004 (p.174)
Digital C–Type Prints
Collection of the Artist

George Vincent (1796–1832)
Dutch Fair on Yarmouth Beach 1821 (p.160)
Oil on canvas 1112 × 1435
Norfolk Museums and Archaeology Service
(Great Yarmouth Museums)

George Stubbs (1724–1806)
Otho, with John Larkin up 1768
Oil on canvas 1013 × 1270
Tate. Presented by Paul Mellon through
the British Sporting Art Trust 1979

THE MYSTICAL WEST

David Cox (1783–1859)
A Welsh Funeral, Betws-y-Coed c.1847–50
(p.208)
Oil on paper 540 × 749
Tate. Purchased 1936

William Overend Geller (1804–1881)
The Druid's Sacrifice 1832 (p.197)
Mezzotint 270 × 380
Salisbury and South Wiltshire Museum

Thomas Guest (1754–1818)
Grave Group from a Bell Barrow at Winterslow
1814 (p.194)
Oil on canvas 453 × 607
Salisbury and South Wiltshire Museum

Barbara Hepworth (1903–1975)
Pelagos 1946 (p.216)
Part painted wood and strings
430 × 460 × 385 15.2 kg
Tate. Presented by the artist 1964

James Dickson Innes (1887–1914)
Arenig, North Wales 1913 (p.210)
Oil on wood 857 × 1137
Tate. Presented by Rowland Burdon–Muller 1928

Thomas Jones (1742–1803)
The Bard 1774 (p.204)
Oil on canvas 1155 × 1677
National Museums & Galleries of Wales

Laura Knight (1877–1970)
Spring 1916–20 (p.185)
Oil on canvas 1524 x 1829
Tate. Presented by the Trustees of
the Chantrey Bequest 1935

Peter Lanyon (1918–1964)
Thermal 1960 (p.217)
Oil on canvas 1829 × 1524
Tate. Purchased 1960

Richard Long (born 1945)
Cerne Abbas Walk 1975 (p.190)
Ink, printed text and photograph on
map and photograph
724 × 737 support: 359 × 537
Tate. Purchased 1976

Edward McKnight Kauffer (1890–1954)
Stonehenge 1931 (p.196)
Poster
Victoria and Albert Museum, London

John Minton (1917–1957)
Recollections of Wales 1944 (p.211)
Ink and bodycolour on paper 495 × 630
British Council

Paul Nash (1889–1946)
Equivalents for the Megaliths 1935 (p.195)
Oil on canvas 457 × 660
Tate. Purchased 1970

Ben Nicholson (1894–1982)
1943–45 (St Ives, Cornwall) 1943–5 (p.215)
Oil and pencil on canvasboard
406 × 502
Tate. Purchased 1945

Samuel Palmer (1805–1881)
The Waterfalls, Pistil Mawddach, North Wales
1835–6 (p.206)
Oil on canvas 406 × 260
Tate. Purchased 1968

Eric Ravilious (1903–1942)
The Vale of the White Horse c.1939 (pp.183, 188)
Pencil and watercolour on paper 451 × 324
Tate. Purchased 1940

Graham Sutherland (1903–1980)
Black Landscape 1939–40 (p.187)
Oil and sand on canvas 810 × 1321
Tate. Purchased 1980

J.M.W. Turner (1775–1851)
*The Chancel and Crossing of Tintern Abbey,
Looking towards the East Window* 1794 (p.201)
Pencil and watercolour on paper 358 × 255
Tate. Bequeathed by the artist 1856

After J.M.W. Turner (1775–1851)
Stone Henge, Wiltshire engraved by
Robert Wallis 1829 (p.182)
Engraving on paper 166 × 234
Tate. Purchased 1986

Alfred Wallis (1855–1942)
*'The Hold House Port Mear Square Island Port
Mear Beach'* ?c.1932 (p.212)
Oil on board 305 × 387
Tate. Presented by Dame Barbara Hepworth 1968

Alfred Watkins
The Sacrificial Stone 1924 (p.189)
Photograph
Hereford City Library

Henry Clarence Whaite (1828–1912)
Arthur in the Gruesome Glen c.1908 (p.209)
Oil on canvas 1060 × 1562
Private Collection c/o Peter Nahum at
The Leicester Galleries

William Williams (1758–1797)
Thunderstorm with the Death of Amelia 1784
(p.205)
Oil on canvas 635 × 1019
Tate. Purchased 1962

Richard Wilson (1713–1782)
Llyn-y-Cau, Cader Idris ?exhibited 1774 (p.203)
Oil on canvas 511 × 730
Tate. Presented by Sir Edward Marsh 1945

Snowdon from Llyn Nantlle c.1765–1766 (p.202)
Oil on canvas 1010 × 1270
National Museums Liverpool (The Walker)

FURTHER READING

The number of books about the landscape and landscape art is of course enormous. Some readers may find it helpful, however, to have some directions for further reading and the following short lists give some of the most useful general books, followed by a few more specific to each of the six regions discussed in this book. Some books are more specialised than others and many of them have very full reading lists.

GENERAL

Malcolm Andrews, *Landscape and Western Art*, Oxford 1999
Kenneth Clark, *Landscape into Art*, London 1949
Stephen Daniels, *Fields of Vision: Landscape Imagery and National Identity in England and the USA*, Cambridge 1993
Stephen Deuchar, *Sporting Art in Eighteenth–Century England: A Social and Political History*, New Haven and London 1988
W. G. Hoskins, *The Making of the English Landscape*, London 1955
Ian Jeffrey, *Landscape in Britain 1850–1950*, exh. cat., Arts Council, London 1983
Ian Ousby, *The Englishman's England: Taste, Travel and the Rise of Tourism*, London 2002
Leslie Parris, *Landscape in Britain*, exh. cat., Tate Gallery, London 1972
Oliver Rackham, *The History of the Countryside*, London 1986
Michael Rosenthal, *British Landscape Painting*, Oxford 1982

Simon Schama, *Landscape and Memory*, London 1995
Gilles A. Tieberghien, *Land Art*, London 1995
Ian D. Whyte, *Landscape and History since 1500*, London 2002
Raymond Williams, *The Country and the City*, Oxford 1975

THE ROMANTIC NORTH

David Hill, *Turner in the North. A Tour through Derbyshire, Yorkshire, Durham, Northumberland, the Scottish Borders, the Lake District, Lancashire and Lincolnshire in the Year 1797*, New Haven and London 1997
Karl Kroeber (ed.), *Images of Romanticism: Verbal and Visual Affinities*, New Haven 1980
John Murdoch, *The Discovery of the Lake District* , exh.cat., Victoria and Albert Museum, London 1984
Jonathan Wordsworth, Michael C. Jaye, Robert Woof, *William Wordsworth and the Age of English Romanticism*, exh. cat., New York Public Library, Indiana University Art Museum, Bloomington, Chicago Historical Society 1987–8

THE HOME FRONT

Linda Colley, *Britons: Forging the Nation, 1707–1837*, London, 1992
Eds. David Peters Corbett, Ysanne Holt and Fiona Russell, *The Geographies of Englishness:*

Landscape and the National Past 1880–1940, New Haven 2002
William Vaughan, *British Art: The Golden Age*, London 1999
David Boyd Haycock, *Paul Nash*, London 2002
Allen Staley and Christopher Newall, *Pre-Raphaelite Vision: Truth to Nature*, London 2004

HIGHLANDS AND GLENS

T.M. Devine, *The Scottish Nation, 1700–2000*, London 1999
Murdo Macdonald, *Scottish Art*, London 2000
Alastair J. Durie, *Scotland for the Holidays: Tourism in Scotland, c.1780–1939*, East Lothian 2003, p.47.
John Morrison, *Painting the Nation: Identity and Nationalism in Scottish Painting 1800–1920*, Edinburgh 2003

THE HEART OF ENGLAND

Robert and Monica Beckinsale, *The English Heartland*, London 1980
Asa Briggs, *Iron Bridge to Crystal Palace: Impact and Images of the Industrial Revolution*, London 1979
Stephen Daniels, *Joseph Wright*, London 1999
Mary Greensted, *The Arts and Crafts Movement in the Cotswolds*, Stroud 1993
Francis Klingender, *Art and the Industrial Revolution*, revised ed., London 1968

THE FLATLANDS

Ann Bermingham, *Landscape and Ideaology: the English Rustic Tradition 1740–1860*, London 1987
Andrew W. Moore, *The Norwich School of Artists*, Norwich 1985
Michael Rosenthal, *The Art of Thomas Gainsborough: 'A Little Business for the Eye'*, New Haven and London 1999
Michael Rosenthal, *Constable: The Painter and his Landscape*, New Haven and London 1983

THE MYSTICAL WEST

David Brown, *St. Ives 1939–1964: Twenty Five Years of Painting, Sculpture and Pottery* exh. cat., Tate Gallery, London 1985
Christopher Chippindale, *Stonehenge Complete*, London 2004
Peter Lord, *The Visual Culture of Wales: Imaging the Nation*, Cardiff 2000
Peter Sager, *Wales*, London 1998
Sam Smiles, *The Image of Antiquity: Ancient Britain and the Romantic Imagination*, New Haven and London 1994

ACKNOWLEDGEMENTS

Tate

Stephen Deuchar, Director; Judith Nesbitt, Head of Exhibitions and Displays; Curators David Blayney Brown, Richard Humphreys, Christine Riding; Tim Batchelor, Assistant Curator; Tate Publishing Celia Clear, Roger Thorp, Mary Richards, Emma Woodiwiss; Communications Will Gompertz, Nadine Thompson, Ben Luke; Conservation Jacqueline Ridge, Rosie Freemantle; Registrars Gillian Buttimer, Sarah Wood-Collins; Art Installation Andy Shiel.

BBC

Mark Harrison, Creative Director of Arts; Basil Comely, Executive Producer; Chris Granlund, Series Producer; Paul Ralph, Production Manager; Directors Sally Benton, Jonty Claypole, Robin Dashwood, Nicky Illis, Jamie Muir; Researchers Mark Bates, Rowan Greenaway, Ellen Hobson, Jon Morrice, Anja Scharfenorth; Production Co-ordinators Melanie Hobbs, Alexandra Nicholson; Project Producer Fiona Hill; Press Imogen Carter; Marketing Rachel Budden, Kate Sullivan; BBC Rights Agency Sharon Smith.

THANKS

Brian Allen, Leigh Amor, Conrad Atkinson, Christopher Baker, Sarah Bechtolf, Catherine Brace, Jesse Bruton, David Chipperfield, Ann Chumbley, Julian Cooper, Stephen Daniels, David de Haan, Paul Devereux, Tim Dickson, Rebecca Fortey, Hamish Fulton, Hillary Gerrish, Mary Greensted, Regina Gruber, Robin Hamlyn, Margaret Harrison, Robin Hill, Matthew Imms, Melissa Johnston, Adrian Leharivel, Philip Lewis, Anne Lyles, Henna Nadeem, Quentin Newark, Marguerite Nugent, Barbara O'Connor, Felicity Owen, Michael Richardson, Peyton Skipwith, Selina Skipwith, Sam Smiles, Carolyn Smith, Jane Standen, Chris Stephens, Ben Tufnell, Ian Warrell, Angela Weight, Cheryl Williams, Robert Woof, Patrick Wright.

Page numbers in *italic* type refer to illustrations

First published 2005 by order of the Tate Trustees
by Tate Publishing, a division of Tate Enterprises Ltd,
Millbank, London SW1P 4RG
www.tate.org.uk/publishing

to accompany the BBC TV series *A Picture of Britain*
first broadcast 2005 and
the exhibition *A Picture of Britain* at Tate Britain
15 June – 4 September 2005
Exhibition supported by

TATE MEMBERS

Reprinted 2005

© Tate 2005
Text by David Dimbleby © David Dimbleby 2005

By arrangement with the BBC

BBC © BBC 1996

The BBC logo is a registered trademark
of the British Broadcasting Corporation
and is used under license

British Library Cataloguing in Publication Data
A catalogue record for this book is
available from the British Library

ISBN 1-85437-566-0 (hbk)

Library of Congress Cataloging in Publication Data
Library of Congress Control Number: 2005923325

Designed by Philip Lewis
British Isles drawn by ML Design
Printed in Italy by Conti Tipocolor

TITLE PAGE Thomas Gainsborough (1727–1788),
'Gainsborough's Forest' (*Cornard Wood*) c.1748 (detail)

PAGE SIX River Wye from Symonds Yat Rock